# iPad® for the Older and Wiser

## Get Up and Running with the Apple iPad 2 and the New iPad

### 2nd Edition

Sean McManus

WILEY

A John Wiley and Sons, Ltd, Publication

# Dedication

To Karen

# About the author

**Sean McManus** is an expert technology and business author. His previous books include *Microsoft Office for the Older and Wiser, Social Networking for the Older and Wiser* and *Web Design in Easy Steps*. His tutorials and articles have appeared in magazines including *Internet Magazine, Internet Works, Business 2.0, Making Music, Melody Maker* and *Personal Computer World*. He created Wild Mood Swings (**www.wildmoodswings.co.uk**), a web toy that shows you websites to match your mood, and has a personal website at **www.sean.co.uk**.

# Publisher's Acknowledgements

Some of the people who helped bring this book to market include the following:

*Editorial and Production*
VP Consumer and Technology Publishing Director: Michelle Leete
Associate Director – Book Content Management: Martin Tribe
Associate Publisher: Chris Webb
Executive Commissioning Editor: Birgit Gruber
Assistant Editor: Ellie Scott
Senior Project Editor: Sara Shlaer
Editorial Manager: Jodi Jensen
Editorial Assistant: Leslie Saxman
Copy Editor: Grace Fairley
Technical Editor: Dennis Cohen
U3A Reviewer: Jean Judge

*Marketing*
Associate Marketing Director: Louise Breinholt
Senior Marketing Executive: Kate Parrett

*Composition Services*
Compositor: Carrie A. Cesavice, Melanee Habig
Proofreader: Susan Hobbs
Indexer: Potomac Indexing, LLC

# Acknowledgements

Thank you, as always, to my wife Karen for all her support while I was writing this book, both the first and second editions.

I've had the support of a great team at Wiley on both editions of this book, including Sara Shlaer, Grace Fairley, Dennis Cohen, Ellie Scott, Birgit Gruber, Chris Webb, Kate Parrett, Steve Long, Andrea Hornberger, and Lissa Auciello-Brogan. Jean Judge gave valuable feedback on behalf of the U3A.

For help with research, testing things and mocking up screenshots, thanks also to Kim Gilmour, Mark Turner, Kieran McManus, Peter Döring, Annie Alexander, Neil Cossar, Wylda Holland, Marcus Dawson, Mark Young, Robert Kealey, Wendy White, Annemarie O'Brien and Mark Bennett.

# The Third Age Trust

The Third Age Trust is the body which represents all U3As in the UK. The U3A movement is made up of over 800 self-governing groups of older men and women who organise for themselves activities which may be educational, recreational or social in kind. Calling on their own experience and knowledge they demand no qualifications nor do they offer any. The movement has grown at a remarkable pace and offers opportunities to thousands of people to demonstrate their own worth to one another and to the community. Their interests are astonishingly varied but the members all value the opportunity to share experiences and learning with like-minded people. The Third Age Trust's endorsement of the Older and Wiser series hints at some of that width of interest.

THE THIRD AGE TRUST

THE UNIVERSITY OF THE THIRD AGE

# Contents

**Introduction**    **1**

    What is the iPad?    1

    How this book is structured    3

**Part I – Getting started with your iPad**    **5**

**Chapter 1 – Choosing and buying your iPad**    **7**

    Which generation do you want?    7

    How much storage space do you need?    9

    Connecting to the Internet: Wi-Fi or 4G/3G?    10

    Where to buy your iPad    13

**Chapter 2 – Getting your iPad up and running**    **17**

    Setting up your iPad    17

    Navigating the Home screen    25

    Changing the iPad orientation    26

Contents

Turning the iPad on and off                                  26

Setting up your Internet connection                          27

Making your iPad easier to use                               33

Adjusting other iPad settings                                34

Securing your iPad                                           36

Using the iTunes software on your computer                   37

Introducing iCloud                                           42

Updating your iPad software                                  47

Charging your iPad                                           48

Troubleshooting and fixing your iPad                         50

## Chapter 3 – Keeping notes on your iPad    55

Understanding the Notes screen                               56

Writing your first note                                      58

Dictating notes to your iPad                                 63

Using Auto-text to speed up your writing                     64

Creating your own shortcuts                                  65

Editing your text                                            66

Adding and deleting notes                                    71

Emailing and printing notes                                  72

Searching your notes                                         72

Using the Reminders app                                      75

## Part II – Using your iPad for communications                81

## Chapter 4 – Managing your address book and birthday list    83

Browsing your contacts                          84

Adding contacts to your iPad                     86

Adding birthdays and anniversaries               88

Searching your contacts                          90

## Chapter 5 – Keeping in touch with friends by email          93

Creating an email account                        94

Setting up your email account on your iPad       95

Sending an email                                101

Reading your emails                             105

Managing email folders                          108

Searching your emails                           110

## Chapter 6 – Using FaceTime for video calls                 115

Logging in to FaceTime                          116

Starting a FaceTime call                        117

Talking to a friend with FaceTime              119

Receiving a FaceTime call                       122

Contents

## Chapter 7 – Sending instant messages using iMessage    125

Sending messages                                                        126

Splitting and centring the keyboard                                     129

Managing message alerts through the Notification Centre                 130

## Chapter 8 – Browsing the web on your iPad    135

Entering a website address                                              136

Using the Search box                                                    139

Zooming the page                                                        140

Scrolling the page                                                      141

Using links on websites                                                 143

Entering information into websites                                      144

Browsing multiple websites at the same time in tabs                    145

Managing bookmarks, history and web clips                              148

Sharing website content                                                154

Using Reader to make it easier to read pages                           155

Using Private Browsing mode                                            156

## Part III – Sound and vision    161

## Chapter 9 – Adding music and video to your iPad    163

Browsing the iTunes store                                               164

Buying music and video from iTunes                                     167

Using the iTunes store on your computer                                           169

Removing content and downloading it again                                    170

Adding CDs to your iPad using your computer                               172

Using iTunes Match to copy music
from your computer to your iPad                                                     174

**Chapter 10 – Playing audio and video on your iPad**     **179**

Playing audio content on your iPad                                                180

Playing podcasts and audiobooks                                                  187

Watching videos on your iPad                                                        188

**Part IV – Getting creative with the iPad**     **197**

**Chapter 11 – Taking and browsing photos
on your iPad**     **199**

Using the cameras on your iPad                                                     200

Viewing photos on your iPad                                                          205

Editing your photos on your iPad                                                     211

Viewing videos on your iPad                                                          213

**Chapter 12 – Adding and managing apps
on your iPad**     **217**

Downloading apps to your iPad                                                      218

Rearranging your apps and web clips                                             222

Deleting apps and web clips                                                          226

Multitasking with apps on your iPad                226

Using multitasking gestures                        227

10 more apps to get you started                    227

## Part V – Using maps and books on the iPad    231

## Chapter 13 – Finding your way with Maps    233

Finding where you are on the map                   234

Getting directions to a friend's house             237

Using Maps to update your address book             241

## Chapter 14 – Reading books and magazines on your iPad    245

Installing iBooks on your iPad                      246

Downloading books using iBooks                     246

Reading books using iBooks                         248

Using the Amazon Kindle app                        250

Using Newsstand to buy magazines                   250

## Glossary    253

## Index    259

# Icons used in this book

Throughout this book, we've used icons to help focus your attention on certain information. This is what they mean:

 Equipment needed — Lets you know in advance the equipment you will need to hand as you progress through the chapter.

 Skills needed — Placed at the beginning of each chapter to help identify the skills you'll need for the chapter ahead.

 Tip — Tips and suggestions to help make life easier.

 Note — Take note of these little extras to avoid confusion.

 Warning — Read carefully; a few things could go wrong at this point.

 Try It — Go on, enjoy yourself; you won't break it.

 Trivia — A little bit of fun to bring a smile to your face.

 Summary — A short recap at the end of each chapter.

 Brain training — Test what you've learned from the chapter.

# PRACTICE MAKES PERFECT

**To build upon the lessons learnt in this book, visit www.pcwisdom.co.uk**

- More training tutorials

- Links to resources

- Advice through frequently asked questions

- Social networking tips

- Videos and podcasts from the author

- Author blogs

# Introduction

**Equipment needed:** Just this book, and your iPad if you already have it.

**Skills needed:** Some curiosity about the iPad and what it can do for you.

## What is the iPad?

The iPad (see Figure 0.1) is a portable computer, made by Apple. It is based on a touchscreen, which means the screen can detect when you're touching it so you don't need any other input devices. Instead of using a mouse to move a cursor around, you use your finger to touch what you want on the display screen. Rather than typing on an actual keyboard, you touch the keys on a picture of a keyboard on the screen. You slide your fingers across the screen to move items around and use a host of other 'gestures', or finger movements, to issue commands. It's a completely different way of working and having fun. Like driving a car, it takes a little time to learn the controls but before long you are able to control the device without thinking about it.

The iPad is ideal for older and wiser computer users for a few reasons. Firstly, it includes all the software you need for using the web, keeping in touch with friends, browsing photos, watching videos, listening to music, reading books, managing your address book, taking notes and viewing maps. That covers pretty much everything you're likely to want to do often with a computer. On top of that, it's extremely lightweight, so you can use it comfortably anywhere. The screen is easy to see, and you can magnify websites and photos to get a clearer view. The size of the screen also means the icons are well spaced out, so it's easy to control the device by touch. The iPad can be enhanced with free or cheap software applications covering virtually any hobby or interest you might have taken up in retirement, and Apple makes it easy for you to find and install these, as you'll see.

The iPad is ideal for relaxing on the sofa or for taking out and about with you. At about 9.5 inches long by 7.5 inches wide, it easily fits in your bag. Depending on what you're doing with it, Apple says you can use the iPad for up to 10 hours before you have to find a plug socket to recharge its battery. Some models of the device even include satellite positioning so you can use it to navigate in the car (from the passenger seat, of course!).

Copyright © Apple Inc.

**Figure 0.1**

The iPad is one of many touchscreen devices that are known as tablet computers. Its slick design has inspired the market like no other, though. The iPad was first launched in April 2010 and it took just a month to sell a million of them and 12 million programs to run on it (called 'apps').

Apple supports the iPad with a number of services, including the iTunes store, which sells music and video; the iBookstore, which sells books you can read on your iPad; and the App Store, which sells software for your iPad. There are now over 200,000 apps designed for the iPad, and the iPad is also compatible with most of the 500,000 software applications created for the iPod touch and the iPhone, Apple's pocket-sized touchscreen devices.

> The iPad and the iPod are not the same thing. The iPod is a pocket-sized device, originally created for playing music. The iPod touch, one of several devices in the iPod line, has many of the same functions as the iPad but is much smaller.

Some people might be worried about the iPad because it's so completely different to what they're used to. If that sounds like you, the good news is that the iPad is much simpler to use than a desktop computer. Apple has a reputation for creating products that users find quick to learn and intuitive to use, and this book will introduce you to the important features so that you can get started quickly.

You soon learn to love the flexibility and immediacy of the iPad. It can be taken anywhere, and it wakes up from its sleep mode immediately so you can use it on impulse when you think of something you want to email, Google or watch. Most of the time, you'll find the iPad does exactly what you want, with much less fuss than the typical computer.

## How this book is structured

This book takes you through the whole process of discovering the iPad. It's divided into five parts:

● Part I is about getting started with your iPad. You'll learn about the different iPad versions you can choose from, how to buy it and how to set it up. You'll also learn how to use your first app to keep notes and how to navigate the iPad's apps and settings.

● Part II is all about using your iPad for communications. The iPad is ideal for activities such as web browsing and emailing, and also has a great address book and diary function. I'll show you how to exchange instant messages with friends who have compatible Apple devices.  If you have an iPad with built-in cameras, you'll learn how to conduct video calls.

● Part III is about sound and vision. You'll learn how to buy music and videos from Apple's iTunes store, how to watch films and listen to music, and how to copy your music CDs into your iPad. In this part, you'll also discover how to create playlists of your favourite songs.

● Part IV shows you how to unleash your creativity using the iPad. You'll learn how to view your photos on your iPad, and how to expand your iPad by adding new software from the App Store. If you have an iPad with cameras, this part of the book will show you how to take photos and shoot videos using your iPad.

● Part V shows you how you can view maps and books on your iPad. You'll learn how to find your way using the Maps app that is included with your iPad. There's a huge selection of books and magazines available to read on your iPad, too, and I'll show you how you can find them, add them to your iPad and read them.

As you work through the book, you'll build on some of the skills that you learn earlier on. I recommend you read the book in the order in which it's written, but I'll provide reminders and cross-references as appropriate, for those who prefer to jump around the chapters. There is also a glossary and an index you can use to refer back to anything you might have missed or forgotten.

Visit **www.pcwisdom.co.uk** or my website at **www.sean.co.uk** for bonus content and additional information.

# PART I
## Getting started with your iPad

Writing notes on this is a piece of cake.
—All you need is a fine magic marker.

# Choosing and buying your iPad

**1**

**Equipment needed:** A credit card!

**Skills needed:** None, but computer-buying experience might make this easier for you.

Once you've decided to buy an iPad, you have a few more decisions to make. There are several different versions of the iPad, and where you can buy it will depend on which version you want to get.

The main decisions you need to make are: whether to buy the latest product or look for an older device; how much storage space you need; and how you want to connect to the Internet (by using Wi-Fi only, or by using a mobile communications network as well). In this chapter, I'll talk you through these choices.

## Which generation do you want?

There have been three generations of the iPad:

● The original iPad, released in April 2010. It's later been referred to as the iPad 1, but when it first came out, it was just called 'the iPad'. If your iPad doesn't have cameras, then you have an iPad 1. If you have one of these first generation iPads, you can still use nearly all the features described in this book, including the software for viewing photos.

- The iPad 2, which was released in March 2011, introduced a few new features. Two cameras were added, one on the front and one on the back. This iPad also featured a Smart Cover (sold separately), which folds up into a stand so your iPad rests at a comfortable angle for typing or for watching the screen. When you close the cover over the screen, the iPad goes to sleep and when you open it again, it instantly comes back to life. The only weakness is that the cover doesn't protect the back of your iPad.

- The third generation iPad, which was released in March 2012. This has all the features of the iPad 2, including the Smart Cover (still sold separately). Text and images are much sharper and high-definition videos can be played at their full quality on the new iPad's improved screen, which Apple calls a 'Retina Display'. The camera was greatly improved and Apple added the ability for your iPad to take dictation from you, so you can speak text instead of typing it. The iPad 1 and iPad 2 both enabled 3G mobile communications, but the new iPad includes support for 4G, the fastest mobile communications network. I'll explain this further shortly.

When Apple releases a new iPad, it often adds some new software features. You can add some of these features to older iPads for free by updating your software. See Chapter 2 for more details.

When you buy an iPad from a shop, you'll usually be sold the latest generation. If you're buying just after a new generation has been launched, you might be able to pick up the previous model at a discount while stocks last. Apple also sells refurbished older iPads from its website (**www.apple.com**), and there is a healthy second-hand market in such a hot gadget, of course. If your budget can take the strain, though, it's usually worth buying the latest model.

Whichever generation iPad you use, most of the information in this book will apply to you and I'll let you know if there are any significant differences you should be aware of.

# How much storage space do you need?

You can't add extra storage space to your iPad later, in the way you can add space to a desktop computer by connecting a new hard drive or other storage device, so before you buy your iPad you need to decide how much space you're going to need.

The iPad is available with three different capacities: 16GB, 32GB and 64GB. (GB is short for gigabyte, a unit for measuring how much information fits on a device or disk.) How much is that? Well, one gigabyte is enough to store about 10 hours of music bought from Apple or an hour of film (half that if it's high definition). You'll get about 220 songs to a gigabyte if you copy your own CDs using the Good Quality setting (which is lower quality than iTunes downloads, but good enough for small speakers). My 7 megapixel digital camera gets about 400 photos to a gigabyte, but your camera might have larger or smaller files depending on whether it has a higher resolution (for example, 12 megapixels) or lower. The camera on the third generation iPad is 5 megapixels, so you can get over 600 photos to a gigabyte, depending on what you photograph. Books vary greatly in size; you might get as many as 1000 text-only books (including novels) or just 40 illustrated books to a gigabyte. These are all just rules of thumb, though. You'll get a lot fewer songs to a gigabyte if you're into prog rock songs with 13-minute guitar solos, for example.

The storage space is also used up by apps, which differ a lot in size, from negligibly small up to about a third of a gigabyte for those that are rich in sound and images. If you want to put your own documents on your iPad, these will be drawing on the same pool of storage space, too.

Apple uses some of the storage space for its own software and memory, so there is less space for you to use than the advertised device capacity. A 16GB iPad only has 14GB you can use, for example. Don't buy an iPad with just enough space. Leave room for Apple's software – and for your music or photo collection to grow.

It's not hard to see how the space can fill up after you've used the iPad for a while, especially if you want to download lots of films. A 16GB iPad might have enough space for three films, a few large apps and lots of small ones, 40 music albums, and a few hundred photos. A desktop computer costing about the same as an iPad might have ten or more times as much storage space, so there's less space on the iPad than you're used to having.

That said, it's important to remember that you can change the music, videos, apps and photos on your iPad regularly. It isn't designed to store all of your files all of the time. You might change the films or TV programmes when you've watched those that are currently on your iPad, or put new music on and take some old music off when you fancy a change. Apple's iCloud service enables you to download music, videos and apps again if you delete them from your iPad, and you can also use your computer to store content and then copy it to your iPad when you want to use it.

If you already have a music or photo collection that will fit on one of the higher capacity iPads, you might want to buy one of those. You'll pay more for the higher capacity devices, but they are priced so that the increased capacity is a relatively small investment. At the time of writing, you can double your storage space from 16GB to 32GB by spending 20% more on your iPad. (You can find current prices at **www.apple.com/uk**). I bet a lot of people have been seduced by Apple's pricing into buying a bigger capacity iPad than they originally planned to. You can justify splashing out more because it will save you time moving files around later, particularly if you're a movie buff and you want to carry your favourite films wherever you go.

If you don't already have a music or photo collection on your PC that you want to be able to store in its entirety on the iPad, you might well find that 16GB is enough for your needs. Some people never fill that, and activities like watching YouTube videos, emailing and using the web have little or no impact on your storage space.

## Connecting to the Internet: Wi-Fi or 4G/3G?

There are two different types of Internet connection that the iPad can support: Wi-Fi and mobile communications.

All iPads can use Wi-Fi. This is a way of connecting to the Internet wirelessly that works in a small area, such as in an Internet café, or in your own home if you have a Wi-Fi router for your broadband connection. It's usually free for you to connect to public Wi-Fi, but places like hotels sometimes charge for access. Wi-Fi has the advantage of being faster than mobile communications networks, but has the drawback of only being available in some areas, and in a fairly small radius in those areas.

For every generation of the iPad, there is also a more expensive version that can use mobile communications. This works a bit like a mobile phone in that you can connect anywhere you can get a mobile signal, but you have to buy a data plan (basically, a contract) from a mobile phone company to be allowed to use their network. Note that although you'll buy your data plan from a mobile phone company, the iPad isn't designed to support voice calling, although you can use Face-Time for video calling (see Chapter 6) and you can add a Skype app for communications (see Chapter 12 for advice on adding apps).

The original iPad and the iPad 2 supported a type of mobile communications called 3G, short for 'third generation mobile communications', which is widely used in the United Kingdom. The new iPad uses the much-faster 4G technology, which is only available on a limited and experimental basis in the UK, but is taking off in the United States. If you don't have 4G in your area, the new iPad will use the best available alternative (typically 3G). You have a free choice of companies you can buy your data plan from, but not all mobile phone companies support the iPad. At the time of writing, in the UK you can get a contract from O2, Three, Orange or Vodafone. When you sign up with one of these companies, they will send you a micro SIM card to insert into your iPad, or you can request one from Apple if you buy your iPad directly from them. The micro SIM card is a different size to the SIM cards used in mobile phones, so you can't just swap one with your mobile phone.

Unlike with a mobile phone, you don't need to have a long-term contract. While many of the contracts re-bill automatically at the end of each month, you can typically cancel at any time and start up again later. You might just want to buy a month's network access for your summer holiday and then cancel it when you return, for example. Daily and weekly contracts are also available, so you don't have to buy a full month's worth of access.

The contracts allow you to download a certain amount of data over the network within a certain timeframe. O2, for example, offers a contract that gives you 1GB of data to download within 30 days, which amounts to about 200 songs, two hours of video or 10,000 web pages (according to O2's own estimates).

Data just means information. It includes maps, web page content, music, videos and anything else you get from the Internet.

The data plans sometimes provide free access to subscription-based public Wi-Fi hotspots too. This can help your data allowance to go further because you can download as much as you like over Wi-Fi, in public or at home. It's only the content downloaded using the mobile communications connection (3G or 4G) that's restricted.

Check the Apple website for the latest data plans and providers.

The 3G and 4G iPads also have GPS, a positioning system that uses a network of satellites to work out where you are. If you want to use maps extensively, this can be extremely useful, although there are more basic (and less accurate) positioning features in the Wi-Fi iPad too.

Whether you need a Wi-Fi-only iPad or one that also supports mobile communications will depend on how you intend to use it. If you want to use your iPad mainly at home and you have a Wi-Fi router at home, then the Wi-Fi version will be perfect. Most of its features will work wherever you are, but you won't be able to download new content from the Internet or from the iTunes store unless you connect to a Wi-Fi network. You'll have fast Internet access through your own Wi-Fi connection while at home, and will also be able to connect to the Internet at many big name and independent cafes, libraries, universities, and other institutions all over the world.

If you want to ensure you can connect to the Internet from almost anywhere (depending on the availability of the mobile communications network), then the 3G/4G iPad might be for you. It costs more than the Wi-Fi version to buy, however, and you'll have to pay additionally for access to the mobile communications network. The 3G/4G iPad is the natural choice for somebody who travels a lot, especially within the UK, or for someone who wants to make extensive use of the maps feature on the road. It might be expensive to use 3G or 4G roaming abroad, although you might be able to buy a data plan in the country you are visiting to cut the cost. It's easy to burn through your data allowance on mobile communications, especially if you have access to a superfast 4G network. You can turn off mobile communications until you need it (see Chapter 2), though, to make sure you're only using your data allowance when you choose to.

If you do opt for a 3G or 4G iPad, it will use Wi-Fi instead wherever that is available, to save you using up your data allowance unnecessarily.

## Where to buy your iPad

The iPad is a hot gadget, so lots of shops want to stock it. There's probably somewhere near you that sells it, and where you might even have the opportunity to try it out before you buy.

Apple has its own shops in major cities and towns, where you can get expert consultancy on your purchase. Figure 1.1 shows the Apple Store on the upper west side of New York City. The store usually has Apple devices set up that you can just go in and play with, so it's the perfect place to get a feel for the device before making your decision. The team in the store can also pre-install a micro SIM card for you if you want, which will save you a slightly fiddly job later (see Chapter 2) if you're buying a 4G iPad.

Apple also sells online (with free engraving available) and by phone. Visit **www. apple.com** for store details, the phone number and online shopping. The downside of buying direct from Apple is that you won't get a discount, because Apple won't want to compete unfairly with its retail partners.

**Figure 1.1**

Other consumer electronics stores and mobile phone stores also sell the iPad. Mobile phone stores might only sell the 4G version with a contract, so if you want a Wi-Fi version it's best to look elsewhere. If you do buy from a mobile phone shop on a contract, study the small print. The iPad will often be heavily discounted, but that's because you sign a contract to pay a monthly 4G fee for two years. Those deals work out well for business travellers who use their iPad heavily, but probably won't be ideal for someone who will mostly use their iPad at home or other places where Wi-Fi is available. As I said before, you can use a 4G iPad and just pay for a month or so of 4G access when you're on holiday, so you don't have to sign a contract and pay every month.

Major online retailers, including Amazon, also sell the iPad and their prices are sometimes lower than those typically found in the high street.

You can find a guide to the various accessories available for the iPad, such as cases, power adapters and screen protectors, at **www.pcwisdom.co.uk**.

## Summary

- There are three generations of iPad. The iPad 2 introduced two cameras and the third generation iPad has a much higher screen quality than previous iPads.

- The iPad is available with storage capacities of 16GB, 32GB and 64GB.

- You can't upgrade the memory of your iPad later, so make sure you pick one that's big enough now.

- You can swap around the files you store on your iPad easily, so it doesn't matter if they don't all fit at once.

- All iPads can use free Wi-Fi to connect to the Internet, including through your wireless router at home if you have one.

- Some iPads also enable 3G or 4G communications. You have to pay more to buy one of these devices, and have to pay for using the mobile communications network.

- Wi-Fi offers a connection within a small area, such as in a café or in your home. 3G or 4G is more like the connection for a mobile phone and can be used wherever there is a 3G or 4G signal.

- You can buy your iPad direct from Apple, from a mobile communications company or from a consumer electronics store.

# Brain Training

At the end of each chapter of this book, there's a short quiz to refresh the points covered and give you a break before the next chapter. Sometimes there's more than one right answer.

**1. Wi-Fi is:**

(a)   A wireless Internet connection

(b)   A companion for Hus-Bandi

(c)   A type of mobile phone

(d)   A high tech way to order coffee

**2. A 4G iPad is:**

(a)   One that is moving incredibly fast

(b)   One that costs £4,000

(c)   One that can use a mobile communications network to access the Internet

(d)   One that weighs the same as a few paperclips

**3. To store the most films, music, photos and apps on your iPad, you need one with:**

(a)   16GB

(b)   32GB

(c)   64GB

(d)   4G

**4. The best iPad for mapping is:**

(a)   The 3G or 4G version

(b)   The Wi-Fi only version

(c)   The original iPad

(d)   The iPad 2

**5. You can use the iPad Smart Cover to:**

(a)   Turn off your iPad

(b)   Prop up your iPad to watch videos on it

(c)   Prop up your iPad for typing

(d)   Protect the back of your iPad

## Answers

**Q1** – a    **Q2** – c    **Q3** – c    **Q4** – a. Both 3G and 4G iPads have GPS built-in.    **Q5** – a, b and c

# Getting your iPad up and running

2

**Equipment needed:** An iPad. Ideally, a broadband Internet connection and a Wi-Fi router set up at home. A micro SIM card, if you have a 4G or 3G iPad.

**Skills needed:** None, but experience installing software is helpful.

You've ripped off the packaging, admired the shiny screen and you now want to start playing with your iPad. The bad news is that you need to spend a little bit of time setting it up before you can do anything with it. The good news is that – if your experience is anything like mine – it's easier to set up your iPad than it was to get it out of the shrink-wrap. In this chapter, I'll guide you through the process of setting up your iPad. You'll also get a first glimpse at how it works, and will be able to configure it so that it's as easy to use as possible. I'll also show you how you can copy information between your computer and iPad using the iCloud service or the iTunes software on your computer.

## Setting up your iPad

Your iPad should arrive charged, so you can start setting it up straight away. If you can't get a response out of your iPad, or it shows you a dead battery image, jump ahead to the instructions on charging your iPad later in this chapter, and then double-back here to continue setting up. The iPad uses its touchscreen for almost all of its controls, so there are very few buttons on it, as you can see on Figures 2.1 and 2.2. Because of the bevelled edge, most of the buttons aren't visible from the front, so I've flipped the iPad over to show where they are, although you can use them all while looking at the screen.

Front camera

Home button

**Figure 2.1**

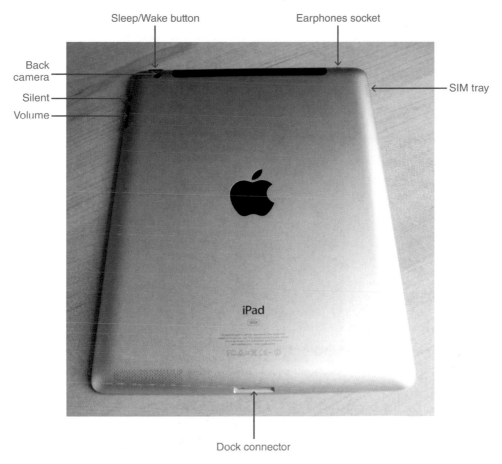

**Figure 2.2**

It doesn't usually matter which way up you use your iPad, but to set it up, you need to hold it so that the round button (the Home button) on its front surface is at the bottom. On the top edge of the iPad, on the right when you look at the screen, you can find the Sleep/Wake button. Press and hold the Sleep/Wake button and you will see the word 'iPad' shown on the screen.

Towards the bottom of the screen is the first touchscreen control you will use (see Figure 2.3), the slider. Beside it are instructions which cycle through lots of different languages. Put your finger on the arrow and move your finger to the right, keeping it in contact with the glass all the time. As you move your finger, the arrow will move with it. When it reaches the right edge of its box, release your finger and your iPad will be unlocked.

**Figure 2.3**

For the next step, you'll need one of the simple gestures used to control the iPad, the tap. On a touchscreen, tapping something is a bit like clicking it with a mouse on a desktop computer. To tap something, you just touch it briefly and then lift your finger from the iPad. This gesture is often used to select things on the screen, or to push 'buttons' on the screen, which are just symbols or words that do something when you touch them.

Use the skin of your fingers, not your fingernails. It's easiest if you use the surface of your fingers where your fingerprints are. You don't have to press the screen. Just touch it.

The first thing you'll select by tapping is your language. If you're happy with the one that's been chosen for you by default, shown at the bottom of the screen, tap the blue arrow in the top right. If not, tap the arrow at the bottom of the screen to see a list of available languages. You can scroll this list by putting your finger on it and dragging it up and down the screen. When you find your preferred language, tap it, and then tap the blue arrow in the top right. It will take a moment to set your language. You use a similar process to choose your country or region in the next step, tapping Next in the top right when you have chosen your country (indicated on Figure 2.4).

You'll be asked whether the iPad should enable location services. If you enable location services, you will allow some of the software on your iPad to know your iPad's location. This is a big help when you're using Maps (see Chapter 13) or taking photographs (see Chapter 11), so I recommend you enable location services and then again tap Next.

The next step is to set up your Wi-Fi connection. Wi-Fi is a way of connecting computers and other devices wirelessly to the Internet and to each other. It's a great idea to set up a Wi-Fi network at home if you haven't already, so that you can easily access the Internet on your iPad wherever you are in the house. If you don't have a Wi-Fi network at home, you can set up your iPad using a friend's network or a public Wi-Fi network in a café or library.

If you don't have a Wi-Fi network available, tap Connect to iTunes, tap Continue, and then follow the instructions in the section 'Using the iTunes software on your computer' later in this chapter to install the iTunes software (if necessary) and connect your iPad to your computer. You will be asked to give your iPad a name, and to decide whether to automatically synchronise (copy) songs, photos and apps to your iPad. Later in this chapter, I will explain synchronising your iPad with your computer. Once you've answered these questions on your computer, return to your iPad to continue setup.

To set up a Wi-Fi connection on your iPad, you will need the name of the Wi-Fi network and its password. If you're using your own router, you can find out or change the password by checking your router settings. If you are using public Wi-Fi, you will usually be given the network name and password together.

If there is a Wi-Fi network nearby, you'll be asked to select it and then enter its password. If there are several networks nearby, you might have to choose your network from among them. Choose a network to connect to by tapping its name. A keyboard will appear (see Figure 2.4) on the touchscreen so you can enter the password for the Wi-Fi network by tapping the keys on screen. When you type a password, you can only see the latest character entered for a moment, so keep an eye on the characters as you type to make sure there aren't any errors. To enter a number or symbol, tap the key labelled '.?123'. If you hide the keyboard by tapping the key in the bottom right of it, you can bring it back by tapping the password box. You'll learn much more about the keyboard in Chapter 3.

When you type a password on a computer, it just shows up as a line of dots on screen. On the iPad, each character appears on screen for a moment to allow you to check it's correct, so whenever you enter a password, take care nobody with sharp eyes is reading it over your shoulder.

When you've finished entering the password, tap Join, indicated in Figure 2.4. You should see a tick appear beside your chosen Wi-Fi network, showing that it's been set up correctly. You can then tap Next in the top right.

Once the Wi-Fi has been set up or you have completed setup using your computer, you'll be asked to choose to set up your iPad as a new iPad, or to restore it from a backup you made previously of your iPad. (You'll learn more about backing up your iPad later in this chapter.) If this is your first iPad or you don't have a backup of your old iPad, you can just tap Next in the top right. Otherwise, choose the source of your backup (iCloud or iTunes) to copy your backed-up apps and data to this iPad, and then tap Next.

To use many of the features of your iPad, you'll need to have an Apple ID; this is a combination of your email address and a password that you make up yourself. It's used for FaceTime (see Chapter 6), instant messaging (Chapter 7), and to buy things like books, music, films and apps. Apple will ask you to create an Apple ID and will require you to enter credit card details or the number of a gift certificate, which you can buy from many high street shops. The iTunes store uses a secure connection, so your credit card details are safe and cannot be stolen by anyone as they go over the Internet.

You can skip the step of setting up your Apple ID and/or your email address for now if you prefer.

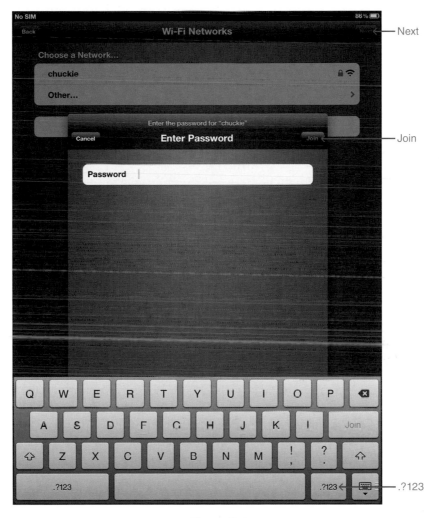

**Figure 2.4**

Apple asks for your birthday so that it can shield you from buying some content you're not old enough to see (not likely to be an issue if you're reading an 'Older and Wiser' book!), and so it can also help you to recover your Apple ID password if you forget it.

You will also have to accept the iPad software licence agreement. This is mainly about the copyright in the content you download to the iPad, such as maps, and also includes clauses about what data Apple collects about you and how it uses it. You can tap each section and scroll through its terms and conditions to read them, but you have to accept them to be able to use your iPad. I'll flag up anything you should be aware of with regards to privacy as you discover new features in this book. When you're happy you're not signing your soul away, tap Agree in the bottom right.

During setup, you'll be asked whether you want to use iCloud or not. This service uses the Internet to back up your iPad and to share its content with other devices you own. When you use iCloud, your files are copied to a private part of the Internet, and your other devices (such as your iPhone or your computer) can copy your files from there. This means you can back up your iPad and can copy files between your computer and your iPad without having to connect them to each other. iCloud is covered in more detail later in this chapter. If you choose not to use iCloud for now, you can easily enable it later, but I recommend that you choose to use iCloud, and use iCloud to back up your iPad over Wi-Fi.

Apple's free Find my iPad service helps you to recover your iPad if it is ever lost or stolen. It enables you to log into a web browser to see where your iPad is on a map, to send a message on the iPad screen to whoever has found it, and even to set a passcode remotely or delete all its contents to stop someone else getting your sensitive data. I recommend you enable this feature. Once your iPad is up and running, you can test it by visiting **www.icloud.com** on a web browser and logging in with your Apple ID. Later in this chapter, you'll learn how to change your iPad settings and you can turn Find my iPad on or off by going into your iCloud settings.

The third generation iPad introduced dictation, which enables you to speak to your iPad instead of typing on its keyboard. I recommend enabling this when you're asked about it. I'll explain the dictation feature more fully in Chapter 3.

In the Diagnostics section, Apple will ask if it can collect information about how you use your iPad, to help it to improve its products. If you're feeling public spirited, you could allow data to be sent automatically. I tend to decline permission for things like this because I prefer to have control over what data is being sent about me and when.

You can choose to register your device to your Apple ID, which means Apple will make a note that you own this iPad. That will speed up any support requests you have and will enable Apple to send you relevant product information.

When you've finished setting up your iPad, Apple will confirm that it's ready to use. Tap Start Using iPad, and the Home screen will appear showing a number of icons (see Figure 2.5).

## Navigating the Home screen

Each activity on the iPad takes place within a software application called an app. On the Home screen, you can see icons for the apps that come installed on your iPad: Messages, Calendar, Notes, Reminders, Maps, YouTube, Videos, Contacts, Game Center, iTunes (a music and film store), App Store and Settings. There's also a special folder called Newsstand, which looks and behaves like an app. On iPads with cameras, you will also see the Camera, Photo Booth and FaceTime apps. To start an app, just tap its icon. At the bottom of the screen, on a shelf called the dock, there are icons for Safari (the web browser), Mail, Photos and Music.

Don't hold your finger on an icon for too long, otherwise you'll go into the mode for arranging icons (see Chapter 12). If the icons start jiggling, press the Home button on the front of your iPad to make them stop.

Try starting the apps to see what they look like. Without any content on your iPad, some of them won't do much, but you can take a quick peek and practise using the touchscreen. When you've finished exploring an app or if you get lost, press the Home button and you'll go back to the Home screen, where you can pick another app.

# Changing the iPad orientation

You can use the iPad any way around. Try rotating it, and you'll see the screen contents rotate too, so that you're always looking at them the right way up. Figures 2.5 and 2.6 show the iPad in the portrait (taller than wide) and landscape (wider than tall) orientations.

As you try different activities with the iPad, you'll find some work more naturally in one orientation than the other. For example, when writing notes or emails, I prefer to use the landscape orientation because it makes the keyboard bigger. You can also rotate the iPad to match the shape of photos (portrait or landscape), so you can see them at their maximum size (see Chapter 11).

Figure 2.6

Figure 2.5

# Turning the iPad on and off

When you're not using your iPad, there are two different states it can be in. Firstly, it can be locked (also known as sleep mode). This might be a bit surprising if you aren't expecting it but, after two minutes of inactivity, the iPad locks itself to save power. You can also force it to lock straight away by pressing the Sleep/Wake button. A locked iPad can still play music and responds to volume controls, but has the screen switched off and won't respond to your touch. To unlock the iPad, press the Home button and then use the slider. Alternatively, if you have a smart cover on your iPad (not available for the first generation iPad), just open the cover. An iPad can be unlocked almost instantly.

The other state your iPad can be in is fully switched off. You could switch off your iPad at the end of the day, although in practice people often just leave their iPad locked so that it will start up more quickly the next time they need it. To turn your iPad off, press and hold the Sleep/Wake button and then drag the red slider to turn it off. You turn it on again by pressing and holding the Sleep/Wake button.

The iPad remembers what you were doing before it was locked or switched off, so all your apps will be exactly where you left them. If you are halfway through an email when your plane is called for boarding, lock your iPad so you can stash it in your bag for now and continue writing later.

# Setting up your Internet connection

In this section, I'll show you how to set up a new Internet connection. You'll need your Wi-Fi network name and password, and your micro SIM from your 4G/3G data provider if you have a 4G/3G iPad. After you've set up your web connection, to see it working, go to Chapter 8 on browsing the web or Chapter 13 on Maps.

## Setting up a Wi-Fi connection

If you followed the steps earlier in this chapter to set up your iPad using Wi-Fi, you will already have a Wi-Fi connection, but you will need to set up others from time to time. You might visit a hotel or a friend's house, for example, and want to use the Wi-Fi there.

After you've joined a Wi-Fi network for the first time, your iPad will join it automatically in future, without asking you for the password. That means your web browsing should be seamless from then on while you're using the same Wi-Fi network (unless the password for the network is changed, in which case you'll be asked to enter it).

To set up a Wi-Fi connection, you need to use the Settings app, which is the engine room of the iPad. It's where you can change lots of different aspects of how the iPad is set up, and how you use it. Go to the Settings app (its icon shows cog wheels) by tapping it on the Home screen. On the left, you can see the different settings you can change. Tap Wi-Fi, and the Wi-Fi settings will appear on the right, as shown in Figure 2.7.

Make sure the switch in the top right says that Wi-Fi is on. You can touch this switch and slide it left or right to turn Wi-Fi on or off. When you see switches like this, you can also just tap them to switch them on or off.

You can then choose a network by tapping its name, and can enter its password, as described in the section on setting up your iPad, earlier in this chapter. Tap Join, and you should see a tick appear beside the Wi-Fi network's name, to indicate you are connected to it.

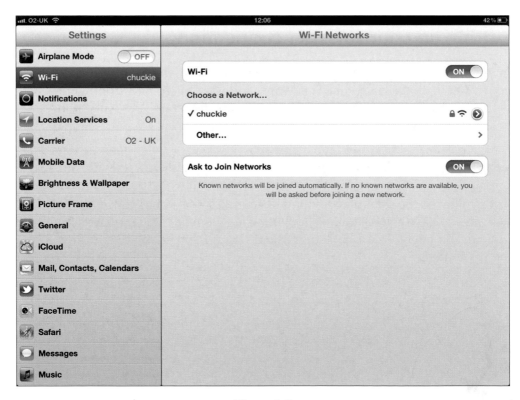

**Figure 2.7**

If you're not connected to Wi-Fi, your iPad will tell if you it comes across other Wi-Fi networks you might be able to join. You won't necessarily be able to join them, though. They might belong to your neighbours or to nearby businesses. If there's a padlock beside the network name, it means you need a password to use it. You can stop your iPad from telling you about networks it finds by turning off the switch beside 'Ask to Join Networks' in the Wi-Fi settings.

## Setting up a 4G/3G connection

As Chapter 1 explained, you can also use mobile communications on your iPad if you have an iPad that supports 3G or 4G. To start using 4G/3G, you need to have a micro SIM card from your data plan provider. If you buy direct from Apple, the company can install the micro SIM for you. If you buy your data plan at a mobile phone shop, they might be able to install your SIM card for you there, too. Otherwise, you'll need to phone or register with a 4G/3G provider online to get them to send you a SIM. If you receive your micro SIM by post, these are the steps you need to follow:

1. Your micro SIM card will probably come in a piece of plastic the size of a credit card. You need to snap the SIM card out of it, to fit it into your iPad. Keep a note of its mobile broadband number, which will look like a mobile phone number.

2. Use the special SIM eject tool that came with your iPad to open the SIM tray on your iPad (indicated in Figure 2.2). When you hold the iPad with the Home button at the bottom, there is a tiny round hole on the left edge. On the original iPad, it's towards the bottom, and on later iPads it's near the top. Insert the tool (or a paperclip will do) in here, and the tray will spring out. Figure 2.8 shows the eject tool being used to open the SIM tray in the side of the iPad.

3. The tray can be completely removed from the iPad. Put the micro SIM card into the tray. It will only go in one way around. If it's too big, check whether there is any more plastic on it that is designed to be snapped off. Remember you can only use a micro SIM card, and not a standard mobile phone SIM card.

4. Carefully replace the tray the right way up. The metallic side of the SIM card that looks like a circuit board should be facing down, away from the iPad's touchscreen.

5. When you turn the iPad on, you'll see a message telling you the iPad is waiting for the SIM to be activated.

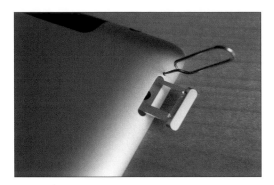

**Figure 2.8**

The next steps you need to take will vary depending on which communications provider you use. For O2, which enables you to sign up on the iPad itself, the steps are:

1. Ensure that you are using the latest version of the iPad software. See later in this chapter for instructions on updating your iPad software.

2. Go into your iPad settings by tapping the Settings app icon on the Home screen.

3. Tap Mobile Data on the left and then tap View Account on the right.

4. Touch each box in turn on the form (see Figure 2.9), and the keyboard will appear so you can enter the information required. Enter your first and last names. The telephone box, confusingly, is not for your phone number. It's for the mobile broadband number that came with your SIM card. You also need to invent a password and enter it twice (to make sure you type it correctly). When you finish entering information in one box, tap the next box on the screen. To scroll the form, touch it and drag your finger up the touchscreen. Touch the data plan (or 'package') you require and tap the Next button at the bottom of the form.

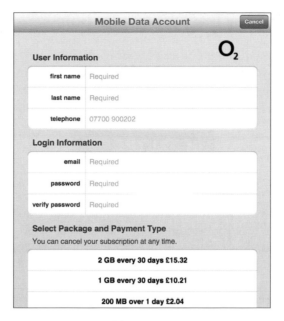

**Figure 2.9**

5. Enter your payment information and address.

6. Read and agree to the terms and conditions. You can scroll the terms and conditions by touching and dragging them.

7. You will see a summary confirming your package and pricing, and when you tap the Submit button, the data plan will be activated.

8. To see how much of your data allowance is still available, go into Settings, Mobile Data, then tap View Account. Note that your remaining data might be shown in MB, and that 1GB is equal to 1024MB.

If you want to use your iPad on a plane, go into the Settings app and turn on Airplane mode (it's the first option in the top left). You just slide its switch to On. This will turn off the radio transmitters and Internet connections so you can use your iPad without interfering with aviation systems.

## Understanding your Internet connection

In the status bar, in the top left corner of your iPad, you can see some icons representing the status of your Internet connection. Much of the time when you're using the Internet, you'll see a fan symbol, which shows that Wi-Fi is working (see Figure 2.10). The more lines there are on the fan, the stronger the Wi-Fi signal is.

**Figure 2.10**

If you have an iPad with mobile communications, you will also see a bar graph indicating the strength of the mobile communications network and the name of your mobile operator. Your iPad will use Wi-Fi whenever it's available and will automatically switch to the mobile network when it's not.

Your iPad will use the best quality mobile network connection available, and you will see a symbol in the status bar to indicate which type of connection you're using. In order of quality, from fastest to slowest, the symbols are LTE, 4G, 3G, E and a round circle. The LTE and 4G connections are only available on third generation iPads, and only in areas that have those networks.

When you see those symbols, you're using up your data plan, so don't go crazy downloading movies! To stop the mobile communications network from being used, go into the settings, tap Mobile Data or Cellular Data and then switch it off.

If you're in a geographic area (such as another country) that your mobile communications provider doesn't cover, the data roaming feature might still enable you to get a connection through another provider. It can be expensive, though, so I recommend you turn that off. You'll find it in the Settings app, under Mobile Data.

Remember that if you're using mobile communications and have a limited data allowance, any web pages, maps, apps, music or videos you download will eat into that data allowance. It's cheaper, and faster, to use Wi-Fi where available.

## Making your iPad easier to use

For those who have impaired vision or hearing, there are several settings that make the iPad easier to use. You can find them by going into the Settings app, tapping General on the left and then tapping Accessibility:

● **VoiceOver:** This reads the iPad screen aloud for the benefit of people who cannot see the screen. It also enables a comprehensive set of gestures for navigating content and entering information. When using the keyboard, for example, you can flick left or right to advance through the keys and have them read aloud. A double-tap enters the character chosen. VoiceOver completely changes the way the iPad is used. I won't be covering it further in this book but if you believe you might benefit from it, the iPad manual provides comprehensive guidance.

● **Zoom:** If you have impaired vision, you can use the Zoom feature to magnify the iPad screen. Once it is switched on, you zoom in by tapping the screen twice in quick succession, using three fingers both times. To change which bit of the screen you are looking at, touch the screen with three fingers and move them in any direction on the glass surface. To increase or decrease the magnification, tap with three fingers and then quickly tap again with those fingers and keep them on the glass. Move your fingers up the glass to zoom in, and down to zoom out. It sounds complicated, but you can practise on the screen for Zoom settings. You can use any combination of fingers and thumbs from any hands. You don't have to use three fingers next to each other if that feels awkward. This feature is really only for those with impaired vision who need to enlarge everything on the iPad's screen, including its buttons. In Chapter 8, you'll learn the pinch gesture, which is an easy way for everyone to magnify web pages and photos.

- **Large Text:** This increases the size of the text in emails and notes. It can be used in combination with the Zoom features, which help you see the other elements of those apps.

- **White on Black:** This reverses the colour scheme so the text is white on a black background. There is a side effect: icons and images also have their colours reversed, so they look like negatives.

- **Speak Auto-text:** If you turn this on, the iPad will speak its text corrections as you type. This is a useful feature for everyone, and works independently of VoiceOver. You'll learn more about this in Chapter 3.

- **Speak Selection:** In Chapter 3, you will learn how to select text. If you switch on Speak Selection, you can choose to have selected text read aloud to you.

- **Mono Audio:** Stereo audio works by delivering different parts of the sound to different ears. Those with poor hearing in one ear might miss part of the sound, so the mono audio setting enables you to hear the complete soundtrack in each ear.

- **AssistiveTouch:** This enables you to carry out complex gestures and activate the iPad's physical buttons using a menu. This enables you to use the iPad together with a joystick, or to carry out gestures that are too difficult for you.

- **Triple-click Home:** This provides a quick shortcut to manage VoiceOver, Zoom, AssistiveTouch or White on Black. When activated, you can press the Home button three times in quick succession to turn them on or off.

## Adjusting other iPad settings

The iPad is a sophisticated device and has many settings you can adjust. Thankfully, you can ignore the vast majority of them, but here are a few you might want to know about:

- **Brightness:** To change the screen brightness, go into Settings and tap Brightness & Wallpaper. Touch the round button and slide it right or left to increase or decrease brightness. The Auto-Brightness setting adjusts the brightness automatically, depending on how much light there is in the room.

- **Wallpaper:** The wallpaper is the image in the background of your iPad's locked and Home screens. To change it, go into your Brightness & Wallpaper settings and then click the iPad picture. You can choose from over 30 images provided by Apple, or from any of your own photos on the iPad.

- **Sounds:** To turn off the sounds when you type on the keyboard, or when you lock or unlock the device or get email, go into your General Settings and then choose Sounds.

- **Volume:** The easiest way to change the volume is to hold the iPad with the Home button at the bottom, and find the 'rocker' switch towards the top of the right edge (indicated in Figure 2.2). This clicks in two directions to turn the sound up or down. There is also a side switch near the volume control that silences sound effects and alerts, but not any music or programmes that are playing. When you use these buttons, the iPad screen shows you the volume change or mute status in the middle of the screen.

- **Reset:** To reset some or all of your settings, go into your General settings and then click Reset. This gives you several options. If you choose Reset All Settings, the iPad's settings will be set to their factory defaults, but your information on the device (including your contacts and music) will be unaffected. If you choose Erase All Content and Settings, your data will be deleted from the iPad and all the iPad's settings will be set to their factory defaults. You can also reset the network settings (including for Wi Fi networks), reset the dictionary (used for Auto-text, which you'll learn about in Chapter 3), reset the Home screen layout (see Chapter 12) and reset location warnings (which are normally presented once for each app that tries to use your location; if you reset the warnings you'll be asked again for each app).

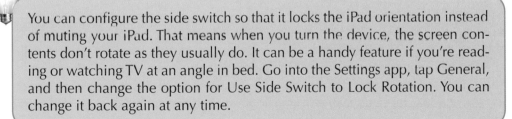

You can configure the side switch so that it locks the iPad orientation instead of muting your iPad. That means when you turn the device, the screen contents don't rotate as they usually do. It can be a handy feature if you're reading or watching TV at an angle in bed. Go into the Settings app, tap General, and then change the option for Use Side Switch to Lock Rotation. You can change it back again at any time.

# Securing your iPad

There are a number of settings you can use to protect your iPad from loss or unauthorised use. Even if you don't have any valuable data on your iPad, these settings can help to protect younger family members from content they shouldn't see online, and to protect your wallet from the risk of them accidentally buying hundreds of apps on your account!

## Adjusting the parental controls (restrictions)

To restrict the content that can be viewed on your iPad, go into the Settings, tap General and then tap Restrictions. Tap Enable Restrictions at the top of the screen and you will be prompted to enter a four digit passcode, twice, just to make sure that it's entered correctly.

You can then restrict access to video conferencing (FaceTime), the web (Safari), Internet videos (YouTube) and Apple's music store (iTunes), and can stop users installing or deleting apps. You can also decide whether to allow the location to be detected in Maps, and whether email accounts may be changed. In-App Purchases enable people to buy content from within an app, and you can restrict explicit music, films with certain certificates, and TV shows and apps unsuitable for younger audiences. There are also settings to stop users playing multiplayer games and adding friends in Game Center, which is an app that comes with the iPad to help you play games with your friends.

To change or disable restrictions again, you'll need your restrictions passcode, so don't forget it!

## Setting a passcode for your iPad

You can protect your iPad from unauthorised access by requiring a passcode to be entered before it can be unlocked. To do this, go into your General settings again, and tap Passcode Lock and then tap Turn Passcode On. As with the passcode for restrictions, the iPad will ask you to enter it twice to make sure you don't mistype it.

If you turn off the Simple Passcode, you can have a longer password using a combination of letters and numbers. The passcode is normally required immediately, but you can set it to be requested after a minute, five minutes, fifteen minutes, an hour or four hours. Allowing a pause of a few minutes might be useful if you want to be able to pop into your iPad to quickly look things up without having to enter the passcode all the time.

You can also set the switch so that all the iPad's content is erased after someone enters the passcode incorrectly 10 times. This helps to protect your data if your iPad is lost or stolen, but isn't recommended for anyone who's ever forgotten a password and has had to keep trying different possibilities!

# Using the iTunes software on your computer

You might already have a computer that you've been using for photos, music, email, contacts and the web. Apple provides two different approaches for copying information from your computer to your iPad. Most obviously, you can connect your iPad to your computer using the USB cable provided. Apple provides free software called iTunes for managing the content on your iPad. If you can't find a Wi-Fi connection to set up your iPad, you'll also need to use this software on your computer to set your iPad up.

Alternatively, you can use the iCloud service, which copies information between your computer and your iPad using the Internet. This service is much more convenient, but if you use a Windows computer, you might find it can't do everything you need yet. I'll cover iCloud later in this chapter, but I recommend you learn about what the iTunes software can do for you too.

## Installing iTunes on your computer

Apple installs iTunes for you on its computers, so this section applies only if you have a Windows computer. The iPad doesn't come with a software disc, so you'll need to download iTunes from Apple's website and then install it.

If you're not comfortable with downloading and installing software, you might want to invite a friend to help with this part. To get the software, you need to use a web browser on your computer, such as Internet Explorer, to visit **www.itunes. com/download**. Complete the form and click the Download Now button. When you're asked whether to Save or Run, choose Run.

During installation, you'll need to decide whether to add shortcuts to your desktop (recommended) and whether to allow Apple to update the software automatically (recommended for security reasons). You can also choose whether to make iTunes the default for playing music on your computer. I don't recommend you select this until you've tried iTunes and decided you'd like to use it all the time. You can change this setting in the iTunes preferences later. Unless you want to change something, it's okay to leave the settings unchanged during installation.

During installation, you'll see a green progress bar go from left to right many times. When the installation is complete, iTunes will tell you and you will need to restart your computer.

## Connecting your iPad to your computer

Now that you have the iTunes software installed on your computer, you can connect your iPad to it.

You'll need the white cable that came with your iPad. It has a different shaped connector on each end. The long, flat plug goes into the iPad's dock connector socket (see Figure 2.2). The opening is on the edge of the device, adjacent to the round button on its front. The plug goes in with the side with the icon to the front of the iPad.

The plug on the iPad cable will only go in one way around, so if you can't get it to fit easily, try flipping the plug over. Don't force it, or you might damage the cable or the socket.

The other end of the cable plugs into a USB port on your computer. You'll often find USB ports on both the back and the front of your desktop computer, or the sides of a laptop, and it doesn't matter which port you use. You might previously have used USB ports to connect your camera, scanner or other device to your computer.

When you connect your iPad to your PC for the first time, a box will pop up on your PC screen to say that a device driver is being installed. When the box confirms your device is ready, you can click the button with the red cross in its top right corner to close the box. An Autoplay box will also open asking you what you want to do with this device. You can ignore this box and just close it in the same way without taking any other action for now.

The iTunes software will then start on your PC. This can take a moment or two, so be patient if it doesn't appear instantly.

If you close iTunes by mistake or it doesn't open for some reason, you can restart it like any other program. If you made no changes to the default options when installing iTunes, you will have an icon on your desktop, which you can double-click. Alternatively, put your mouse cursor over the Start button in the bottom left of your computer screen, click it, click All Programs, click the iTunes folder and then click the iTunes icon.

## Synchronising your iPad with your computer

When you connect your iPad to your computer, the iTunes software synchronises them. That means updates are copied between them, so that new contacts from your computer are added to your iPad, and new photos from your iPad are copied to your PC, for example. If you delete contacts or photos on one device, they might also be removed from the other.

When you connect your iPad to iTunes, you'll see the summary pane, as shown in Figure 2.11.

The central box at the top in Figure 2.11 shows the status of iTunes, and will show you when files are being copied across. Underneath that, you can see buttons to go into the settings for Info, Apps, Tones, Music, Movies, TV Shows, Podcasts, Books, and Photos. Figure 2.11 indicates the buttons for these content types.

iTunes status

Content settings

Capacity graph

**Figure 2.11**

If you don't see your iPad settings in iTunes, select it in the pane on the left. You'll find it listed by the name you gave it under the heading Devices, as you can see in Figure 2.11.

The settings give you a lot of control over which files are copied across. In the music settings, for example, you can choose to copy across all your music, or particular artists, albums or genres. You can also create playlists (which are lists of songs) and choose to synchronise just some of those, so that you have your favourite songs on the iPad, for example, or the songs you've selected for a special occasion. Similarly, if you download podcasts (regular free radio or video shows) on your computer, you can pick individual episodes, or choose to copy a certain number of unplayed episodes to your iPad. Under the Photos settings, you can choose to synchronise selected folders from your computer or choose to synchronise with your photo library in a program like Photoshop Elements. In the Info section, you can synchronise browser bookmarks or contacts from Windows Contacts, Google Contacts or your Yahoo address book by clicking Info.

If you change any of the settings, you'll need to press the Apply button in the bottom right corner to make your iPad synchronise with those new settings. If you change your mind, click the Revert button in the bottom right and iTunes will ignore your changes. These buttons only appear when you change settings.

If you don't want your iPad to synchronise when you connect it to the computer, connect the iPad, and then hold down the Shift and Control keys on your PC keyboard (or Command and Option on the Mac) until the iPad appears in iTunes.

If you've ever spent time trying to work out how on earth you've managed to fill up your computer's hard disk, you'll love this next feature. At the bottom of the screen (see Figure 2.11), you can see a Capacity graph showing how much space is left on your iPad, and how much of each content type you have on it so far.

If you have a lot of music on your computer, there is an alternative to synchronising, called iTunes Match. It is a service that charges an annual fee, but it gives you access to all your music on the iPad. See Chapter 9 for more information.

## Using Wi-Fi to synchronise your iPad with your computer

You can also synchronise your iPad with your computer over Wi-Fi, so you don't need to connect them physically to each other. You'll need to have a computer that uses Wi-Fi, which includes Apple desktops, most modern laptops, and many Windows desktops. To enable Wi-Fi synchronisation, connect your iPad to your computer using the cable and then tick the box for 'Sync over Wi-Fi connection' in the summary pane in iTunes. You will need to scroll the screen to find it. Your iPad will then synchronise with your computer automatically once a day, provided that the iPad is connected to a power source, the computer and iPad are both on the same Wi-Fi network, and iTunes is running on your computer.

## Backing up your iPad using iTunes

If anything should happen to your iPad, it's a good idea to have a copy of the information it contains so that you don't lose that too. It's one thing to lose your favourite gadget, but it can be heartbreaking to lose its photos and all your work too.

You can keep a backup copy of your iPad's data on your computer. In the Summary pane in iTunes, tick the box to back up to your computer. When you synchronise your iPad with your computer, iTunes will copy all the information from your iPad so that if something should go wrong with it, you can recover all your data by resetting the iPad, or copying your backup copy from your computer onto a new iPad. There is also an option to use iCloud for backup, as you'll discover shortly.

# Introducing iCloud

iCloud enables content to be automatically copied between your iPad and other devices without connecting them to each other.

When you use iCloud, your files are copied to a private part of the Internet, and your other devices (such as your iPhone or computer) can copy your files from there. This means you can synchronise much of the content on your iPad with your computer without having to connect them to each other.

## Enabling iCloud on your iPad

You're invited to turn on iCloud when you set up your iPad, but you can change your settings at any time in the Settings app. Go into your Settings and then tap iCloud on the left. Figure 2.12 shows the iCloud settings.

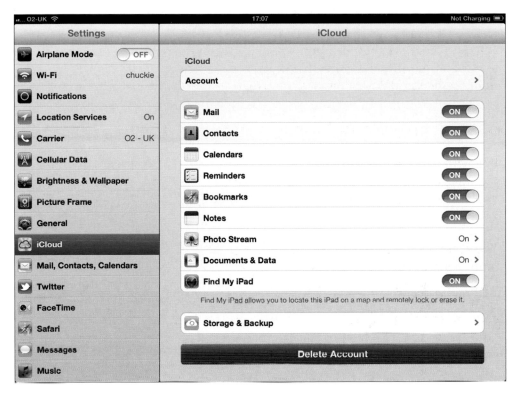

**Figure 2.12**

You can choose which files you would like to synchronise with your other devices, including Mail, Contacts, Calendars, Reminders, Bookmarks, Notes, Documents & Data, and Photo Stream. Documents & Data includes any information created or stored in apps you add to your iPad that are designed to work with iCloud. If you want to synchronise emails and notes, you'll need to register with Apple for a free me.com account (see Chapter 5).

When you use the Photo Stream, any photos you take on your iPad are copied to iCloud and can be automatically downloaded on your computer. You can also upload images from your computer to your iPad automatically. Your photos appear in the Pictures folder on a Windows computer, or in iPhoto or Aperture on a Mac.

Photos are only stored in iCloud for 30 days, so make sure you switch on your computer once in a while to download the photos from your iPad. The iPad, iPhone and iPod touch only keep the last 1000 photos from iCloud, so if you want to stop a photo being removed, go into the Photos app, tap Photo Stream at the top, tap the photo, tap Use Photo in the top right and then tap Save to Camera Roll.

## Using iCloud to synchronise with your computer

You can use iCloud to synchronise your iPad with another iPad, an iPhone, an iPod touch, a Mac or a Windows computer. Not all versions of the iPhone and iPod touch are compatible with iCloud, though, and older devices will need to have their software updated to version iOS 5 or later. There isn't space to go into detail on this here, but you can find out how to update your iPhone or iPod software at Apple's website.

If you have a Mac, you need to update your computer to use OS X Lion v.10.7.2 (or later) and turn on iCloud in your System Preferences. You also need to enable the Photo Stream feature in iPhoto or Aperture.

If you use Windows, you need to have Windows Vista (Service Pack 2) or Windows 7. If you are still using Windows XP, you can't use iCloud on your computer, I'm afraid. To use iCloud on a Windows computer, you need to download and install some free software for your computer from Apple. You can find it at **www.apple.com/icloud/get-started/**. Follow the instructions there to enable automatic downloads, so that any content you buy from Apple using your iPad (such as books, apps and music) is also downloaded to your computer automatically.

To enable content bought on your computer (or other devices) to automatically download to your iPad, go into the Settings app and then tap Store on the left, and switch on automatic downloads for music, apps and/or books.

Figure 2.13 shows the iCloud Control Panel on a Windows computer. You can find it at any time by going through your Windows Start menu. If you click the Photo Stream Options, you can choose where you would like photos coming from your iPad to be stored on your computer. You can also designate an upload folder. Any photos you put into that folder will be copied to your iPad automatically over iCloud. There's no longer any need to mess around with cables to copy photos between your iPad and your computer! You can only copy contacts, mail and calendars, though, if you use the relatively expensive Outlook software on your PC, so you might choose to use the cable to synchronise your contacts from time to time anyway.

**Figure 2.13**

## Using iCloud Backup

If you want to back up your iPad using iCloud, you get 5GB of storage for free and then you can pay a subscription fee to upgrade. Photos in your Photo Stream and content you buy from Apple, such as music, apps and books, don't eat into your 5GB allowance. Any music you didn't buy from Apple that you add to your iPad isn't backed up, so keep a copy of that on your computer using the iTunes software.

To switch on iCloud Backup, go into the Settings app, tap iCloud and then tap Storage & Backup (see Figure 2.12). Your Storage & Backup options will show you how much storage space you have available and how much of it is still free (see Figure 2.14). 5GB isn't that much (you can fit it on a USB key), so you can rent extra storage space if you need it. It costs £14 per year for an extra 10GB of storage, £28 for 20GB or £70 for 50GB. The maximum available space is 55GB (your free 5GB plus a 50GB subscription).

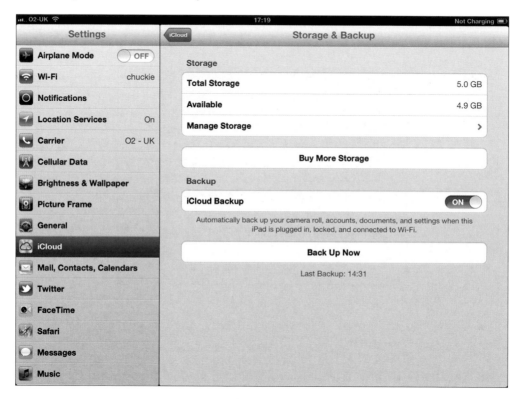

**Figure 2.14**

If you use iCloud Backup, your iPad won't back up to your computer when you synchronise it. Instead, when your iPad is plugged in to a power source, locked and connected to Wi-Fi, your data will be backed up over the Internet to Apple's computers in Maiden, North Carolina. You can also tell your iPad to make a backup at any time by going into the Settings app, tapping iCloud, tapping Storage & Backup and then tapping Back Up Now.

## Updating your iPad software

From time to time, Apple releases a new version of the software on the iPad, which usually improves the iPad's reliability and introduces some new features. The Messages and Reminders apps were introduced as free upgrades for all iPad owners in October 2011, for example. This software update was called iOS 5, and if you have an older iPad, I recommend you update to it now. Some of the apps and features described in this book are only available to those who have upgraded, or who have bought an iPad since the new software was released.

You can update the software on your iPad without affecting any of the information, apps, music or other files stored on it, and the update is a free service. There's usually a lot of press coverage about a significant update, so you can easily find out what you can expect from a particular software update.

There are two ways you can update the software on your iPad:

- Connect your iPad to your computer, and then click the Check for Update button in the iTunes software. You can see this button in Figure 2.11. When iTunes knows an update is available, this button is instead labelled Update.

- On your iPad, go into the Settings app and tap Software Update.

Because Apple updates its software from time to time, you might spot differences between what your iPad does and the behaviour described in this book. Previous updates have tended to introduce new features without dramatically affecting existing ones, though, so any changes are likely to be minor.

You can also update the iTunes software running on your computer. Apple regularly introduces new features and fixes bugs that come to light, especially when it launches a new iPad, iPod or iPhone. In the iTunes software, click Help at the top, and then click 'Check for Updates'.

# Charging your iPad

At the top of your iPad screen is the status bar, which includes information about your iPad and the current time. In the top right corner, you can see the battery indicator. It shows, as a percentage, how charged your battery is. Your iPad will also warn you when the battery gets low.

You can charge your iPad by connecting it to your computer. For this to work, the iPad needs to be in sleep mode and the computer needs to be switched on. Older computers might not be able to provide enough power to charge in this way, though, and even if they can it's relatively slow, so the best method is to connect your iPad to the mains electricity. In the box that your iPad came in, you'll find two parts which slot together to create a standard electrical plug.

The cable provided with the iPad, and which can also be used to connect your iPad to your computer, connects the plug to your iPad. The USB connector (about half the width of the connector on the other end of the cable) slots into the hole on the back of the plug. The other connector slots into the dock connector on your iPad.

When the battery is charging, the battery icon will have a lightning bolt through it.

A fully charged battery has enough juice for most journeys, and you might only need to charge your iPad every few days if you use it around the home. Apple claims that the battery will last for up to 10 hours while using Wi-Fi, watching videos or listening to music. If you use 4G/3G to connect to the Internet, the battery life is cut back to up to 9 hours.

There are steps you can take to prolong your battery life:

- Don't leave your iPad in a hot car and keep it out of the sun. Apple says heat degrades battery performance more than anything else.

- Adjust the brightness to the minimum comfortable level (see 'Adjusting other iPad settings', earlier in this chapter).

- Every month, go through at least one charge cycle, charging the battery to 100% and then running it down completely.

- If your iPad gets hot when charging and you have bought a protective case for it, remove it from its case.

- Keep your iPad software updated. Software updates might include features that help optimise battery use.

- Turn off Wi-Fi and/or 4G/3G when you won't be using them (see earlier in this chapter).

- Minimise the use of location services, such as maps (you can turn off location services in the Settings app).

- Download new emails and other regular updates less frequently. Check fewer email accounts automatically, and turn off features to push email to your iPad (see Chapter 5).

Since the battery wears out over time and can only be replaced by Apple, these tips will also help you to prolong the life of your whole iPad. Apple estimates that you can fully charge and discharge your iPad a thousand times before the battery performance falls below 80% of what it should be. Even if you managed to exhaust your iPad every day, that would give you nearly three years of life, so your iPad is designed to last many years.

You can charge your iPad abroad using the power adapter. You'll need to plug the electrical plug into a travel plug adapter that fits the wall socket of the country you are visiting.

# Troubleshooting and fixing your iPad

If you experience problems with your iPad, there are two things you can do. Firstly, you can check whether there is a software update available for the iPad. It's worth doing this from time to time anyway, because Apple often introduces new iPad features in its software.

If your iPad still appears to be faulty and you can't find a solution online, you can also 'restore' your iPad, as a last resort. This deletes everything from your iPad and reverts its settings to those of a new iPad so you have to start setting it up from scratch. When you set up an iPad, you can choose to recover information from a backup to it.

If you have a recent enough backup, you should be able to restore your iPad without losing information or apps from it, but you'll still have to go through the basic stages of setting up the iPad. To restore your iPad, you can either:

- Connect it to your computer and in the iTunes software click 'Restore' in the Summary pane (see Figure 2.11); or

- Go into the Settings app on your iPad, tap General and then choose Reset. Choose to Erase All Content and Settings and then confirm.

In this part of the Settings app, you can also find options to reset your iPad's settings without deleting any of your files or information from it, to reset the keyboard dictionary, reset the Home screen layout, and reset Wi-Fi network settings.

Now that you've been using the iPad for a while, it will be covered in finger marks. Give it a gentle rub with a cloth for cleaning spectacles. The finger marks look worse when the device is off: when it's on, the screen shines through them no problem. For stubborn marks, Apple suggests a "soft, slightly damp, lint-free cloth" but advises you to take care not to get moisture in the iPad's openings. Never use cleaning agents or abrasives.

## Summary

- To turn on your iPad, press and hold the Sleep/Wake button.

- Use the skin of your fingers on the touchscreen, not your fingernails.

- You can use the iPad any way up, and the screen display will rotate so that it's always the right way up for you.

- iPad activities take place within software applications, called 'apps'.

- You can find icons for your apps on the Home screen.

- Touch an app icon to start the app.

- The Settings app is used to set up your Wi-Fi connection, 4G/3G connection, passcodes and features to improve ease of use.

- To slide a switch on the screen, touch it and move your finger across the iPad screen or simply tap it.

- The iPad has a keyboard that appears on screen when you need to type something in, such as a password. To hide it again, tap the button in the bottom right corner of the keyboard.

- When you type a password on the iPad, each character appears briefly on the screen, so take care that nobody's looking over your shoulder.

- You need access to a Wi-Fi network or a computer to set up your iPad.

- iTunes is free software for your computer that is used to manage the content on your iPad.

- You can use iTunes to copy music, contacts, photos and other content between your computer and your iPad.

- You can also use the iCloud service to copy content between your iPad and other devices without connecting them.

- You can use iCloud or the iTunes software to back up your iPad.

- The best way to charge your iPad is to connect it to the mains.

# Brain training

Now your iPad is set up, you're ready to begin using it. You can refer back to this chapter if you need to change your settings in future, but for now, let's have a quick quiz to refresh your memory. There might be more than one right answer.

**1. You can charge your iPad by:**

   (a)   Connecting it to a power socket

   (b)   Connecting it to a computer, with the computer in sleep mode and the iPad switched on

   (c)   Connecting it to a computer, with the computer switched on and the iPad in sleep mode

   (d)   Connecting it to your computer keyboard

**2. You can use your iPad:**

   (a)   In a landscape orientation

   (b)   In a portrait orientation

   (c)   With the Home button at the top

   (d)   Back to front

**3. When you see an E in the top left of your iPad, it means:**

   (a)   An entertainment app is running

   (b)   You're connected to the mobile network on a 4G/3G iPad

   (c)   You're connected to Wi-Fi

   (d)   That's today's letter on Sesame Street

**4. To protect the data on your iPad, you can:**

   (a)   Delete its contents remotely if it gets stolen

   (b)   Make it delete your data if someone enters the password wrongly 10 times

   (c)   Add a password to stop someone else unlocking it

   (d)   Stop others from deleting apps without a password

**5. To silence the locking sound on your iPad:**

   (a)   Push the Sleep/Wake button really gently

   (b)   Slide the slider on the side of your iPad

   (c)   Adjust your sound settings

   (d)   Put your iPad in a case

## Answers

**Q1** – a and c     **Q2** – a, b or c     **Q3** – b     **Q4** – a, b, c and d     **Q5** – b and c

# Keeping notes on your iPad

**Equipment needed:** An iPad that is ready to use, and reasonably clean fingers!

**Skills needed:** Knowledge of how to start apps (see Chapter 2).

Now that you have your iPad set up and have learned how to navigate its apps, it's time to start using it. In this chapter, you'll learn how to jot down ideas and memos on your iPad. You'll start by using the Notes app, which is one of the simplest apps that comes with your iPad, inspired by a humble pad of paper. Whether you're writing a shopping list, a song or a story, Notes is there in an instant to capture your ideas before they drift away. When you need to refer back to a note, the search function makes it easy to find.

At the end of this chapter, you'll also take a look at the Reminders app, a sophisticated to-do list that includes alerts to make sure you don't forget anything important. Although you can email your notes to people, the Notes app is not intended for creating polished final documents for sharing. There are no features for bold text, underlining, different fonts or any other changes in formatting that you might be used to from a word processing package. At first, that might sound like a limitation, but it's actually a strength: there is nothing distracting or unnecessary on the screen, so you can focus on what you're writing. If you're one of those people who has to fiddle with 15 fonts before you start writing, you're all out of excuses. You don't even have to save your work. Notes takes care of that for you automatically.

You've already seen the keyboard when you were entering passwords to set up your Internet connection. In this chapter, you'll have an opportunity to practise using it and will also see how the iPad's predictive text feature (called Auto-text) can help you to write more quickly.

To start the Notes app, tap the Notes icon on the Home screen.

Although you can't change the text style used for individual notes, you can change the appearance that all notes share. Go into the Settings app and then tap Notes. You can choose from Noteworthy (default), Helvetica and Marker Felt text styles. (On the first version of Notes, the default font was called Chalkboard.) You can enlarge the text size for all your notes to make the text easier to read and select. Go into the Settings app, tap General, tap Accessibility and then choose Large Text. See Chapter 2 for more details.

## Understanding the Notes screen

Notes is a good example of an app that adapts to make best use of the screen space depending on which way up your iPad is. Figure 3.1 shows Notes in portrait mode, where the screen is filled with blank paper. To see a list of your notes, or to search them, you need to tap the Notes button in the top left, as I have in Figure 3.1.

Figure 3.2 shows what Notes looks like in landscape mode. You can see less of each note at a time, but there is a permanent pane on the left that lists your notes and enables you to search them. I prefer the landscape mode because it gives me a bigger keyboard too, so I can type more quickly. You can use whichever orientation suits you best.

When you're using other apps in future, it's worth rotating the screen to see if it declutters the screen or makes additional features easier to find and use.

**Figure 3.1**

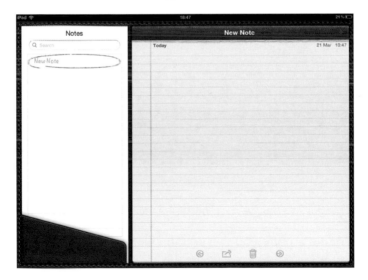

**Figure 3.2**

# Writing your first note

When Notes opens for the first time, it shows what looks like a blank piece of yellow ruled paper. Tap this, and the keyboard will appear so that you can start typing.

Choose your first words carefully: there are no filenames in Notes because your work is saved automatically without any intervention from you. Instead, the first few words you write in a note will be used to refer to it in the list of notes. If you start your note with a short title, such as 'Lasagne Recipe', your notes will be easier to navigate. If your first line reads 'My note about the way to make lasagne', all you'll see in the list of notes will be an unhelpful 'My note about the way…' (see Figure 3.3).

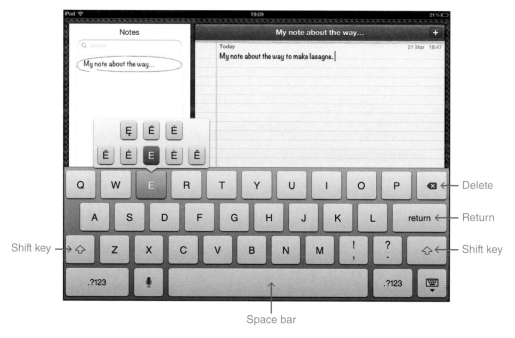

**Figure 3.3**

If you want to retitle a note, you can edit the first line, or insert a new line at the start. You'll learn how to edit text later in this chapter.

## Using the iPad keyboard

Some of the keys on the iPad keyboard are set out in the same way as a normal keyboard. The space bar runs along the bottom in the middle, and the standard QWERTYUIOP layout for letters is present and correct.

In the top right, you can see the Delete key (see Figure 3.3). Tap this to remove a character, or keep your finger on the key to keep deleting, first a character at a time and then a word at a time.

There are two Shift keys, but they work a bit differently to a normal keyboard. You can hold down the Shift key while you tap a letter key to type a capital letter as you would on a normal keyboard, but it might feel a bit awkward. Instead, you can tap a Shift key and then tap a letter. When the Shift key has been activated, the arrow in it turns blue. After you tap a letter, the Shift key is deactivated again.

To speed up your typing, the iPad helps you to start a new sentence with a capital letter. When you finish a sentence with a full stop and a space, the keyboard automatically turns the Shift key on for the next letter. If you forget about this and tap the Shift key, you'll turn it off again so your sentence will start with a lower case letter instead. When the Shift key has automatically been activated for you, the arrow in it is outlined in blue (as you can see in Figure 3.3).

There's no separate Caps Lock key, but if you tap a Shift key twice in quick succession, caps lock is switched on. If the whole of the Shift key except the arrow is blue, it means that caps lock is on and any letters typed will be capitalised until you tap Shift again.

If you tap something twice quickly, it's called a double-tap, a bit like an iPad version of the double-click you might use on a mouse. If the gap between your taps is too long, the iPad might think you made two separate single taps instead, so keep it snappy!

As with a normal keyboard, you can use the Shift key to get different symbols from some other keys. Using Shift with the comma key enters an exclamation mark, for example.

When you reach the end of a line, keep typing and you will automatically be moved to the start of the next line. To start a new line at any time, tap the Return key. You can tap it twice to leave a blank line, to make it easier to see the gaps between paragraphs. When you start a new line, the Shift key is activated so that the first letter will be capitalised. If you don't want that, tap the Shift key to turn it off before you type your first letter.

Don't worry about running out of space on the screen: a note is like a never-ending sheet of paper. You can write as much or as little on it as you want, although you might find it easier to use lots of short notes rather than a few long ones. If your note is too long for it all to fit on the screen at the same time, you can scroll it up or down by touching the note and dragging your finger up or down the screen. The iPad is smart enough to know that if you drag your finger, you didn't intend to tap or select anything on the screen.

You can tap the space bar twice quickly at the end of a sentence to enter a full stop and a space.

## Entering special characters

Using the simple keyboard, you should be able to type shopping lists and simple notes. But what happens when you want to jot down a recipe with all the quantities of ingredients, or need to complete your Spanish homework with all its accents? For situations like this, you need to learn about the more advanced features of the iPad keyboard.

The iPad makes it easier to enter accents than it has been on any other computer keyboard I've owned. If you want to enter an accented character, just tap the letter key and hold your finger on it. A bubble appears above the key, showing the letter with different accents applied (see the E key in Figure 3.3). Without removing your finger from the touchscreen, slide it to the version of the letter you want. When you release your finger, the letter with the accent will be added to your note.

Even if you don't use any foreign languages, this is a useful technique to learn. You can use it on the full stop key to type speech marks, and can use it on the comma key to enter an apostrophe or single quote mark. As you'll see in Chapter 8, it can also help you to enter website addresses more quickly.

There are also two special keyboards you can use to enter numbers and symbols. Tap the '.?123' key and all the keys will change to the keyboard shown in Figure 3.4. This keyboard shows the numbers and most often used punctuation symbols. It also has an Undo key you can use if you make a mistake in deleting or typing text.

Do you remember the Etch-a-Sketch toy that was about the same size as an iPad and enabled you to draw pictures using two dials and delete them again by shaking it? Perhaps as a tribute to that classic toy, you can also undo by shaking the iPad, although it's easier to tap the Undo key.

**Figure 3.4**

As with the letters keyboard, some of these keys have additional symbols that you can find by pressing and holding a key. The £ key, for example, provides quick access to other currency symbols. The apostrophe and speech mark keys provide several different styles (including proper 66 and 99 shaped quote marks). To enter a bullet point, press and hold the dash key until that symbol appears. The full stop key can also be used to enter an ellipsis (three dots in a row).

> If you just want to type one character from this keyboard, there's a shortcut. Touch the '.?123' key and keep your finger on the screen when the keyboard changes. Slide your finger to the key you want to use and then release your finger. Your chosen symbol will be entered and the keyboard will revert to the standard ABC format.

There is a third keyboard that offers a range of less frequently used symbols (see Figure 3.5), such as square and curly brackets, the percent sign, and currency symbols. It also has a Redo key to allow you to reinstate something you undo without meaning to. To show this keyboard, press the '#+=' key that replaces the Shift key on the numbers keyboard (Figure 3.4).

To go back to the letter keyboard from either of the other keyboards, tap the ABC key. To help you type fluently, the iPad automatically switches to the letter keyboard after you type a space or apostrophe.

Figure 3.5

## Hiding the keyboard

The only problem with the keyboard is that it gets in the way of the note itself, which can make it hard to re-read your note. At any time, you can hide the keyboard by tapping the Hide Keyboard key at the bottom right of the keyboard, indicated in Figure 3.5. It's on every version of the keyboard, and you can bring the keyboard back again simply by tapping the note to start typing.

Although it takes a little time to adjust to the feel of the onscreen keyboard, it is possible to type quickly, and Notes provides the ideal place to practise your typing. Give it a go!

## Dictating notes to your iPad

The third generation iPad introduced a new feature that can also speed up your writing: dictation. You can speak to your iPad, and have your words (or, more usually, a close approximation of them) appear on your iPad's screen.

When you use the dictation feature, your speech will be sent to Apple, together with your name, and information about your contacts and songs in your music collection. It's best not to dictate any deep, dark secrets to your iPad, then. Apple's central computers use this information to turn the things you say into the words on your screen. You can turn off the dictation feature in the Settings app (tap General on the left, and then Keyboard on the right).

To use the dictation feature, tap the dictation key to the left of the space bar, indicated in Figure 3.5, which has a microphone on it. Because the dictation service requires the Internet, the dictation key won't appear on the keyboard when you have no Internet connection.

When you tap the dictation key, it will pop out, and will show a noise meter inside the microphone so you can see how well the iPad can hear you. Speak your words of wisdom, and when you've finished tap the dictation key again to end. It takes a moment for the iPad to work out what you've said, and then your words will appear in your note. More likely than not, you'll need to edit your text to correct any words the iPad couldn't correctly make out. Shortly, you'll learn how to do just that.

## Using Auto-text to speed up your writing

You already know about some of the amazing things the iPad can do, but did you know it can predict the future? Okay, so maybe that's stretching it a bit. But it gives it a good go. Try writing the word 'elephant'. You only need to tap four characters before the iPad guesses what you're intending to type, and shows it in a small bubble underneath your typing (see Figure 3.6).

What you're seeing is the Auto-text feature, and you might already have noticed it working while you were entering text before. It's like a cross between the predictive text feature of a mobile phone, and the automatic spelling correction feature of a word processor. It aims to enable you to type more quickly and accurately, but if you're not careful, the iPad can change words you don't want it to.

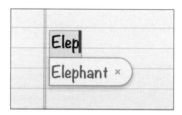

**Figure 3.6**

The word 'book' became slang for 'good' thanks to the predictive text feature of mobile phones, because when you try to enter 'cool' in a text message it often comes out as 'book'.

To accept the iPad's suggestion, just tap the space bar. It doesn't matter how far into the word you are. If the iPad can guess it in four characters, you don't have to type any more.

If the iPad makes an incorrect suggestion, keep typing your word and it will keep trying to guess if it can. Whenever the correct word appears, tap the space bar.

The problem comes if you get to the end of the word, and the iPad thinks you're midway through typing something else or thinks you've misspelled something you haven't. Try typing the word 'ill', for example. When you tap the space bar, the iPad will replace your correct and complete word with 'I'll', which is used more often but which makes no sense in your sentence. To stop this happening, touch the iPad's suggested word on the screen and it will go away. This feels a bit counterintuitive, because usually you touch things to select them, but touching an Auto-text suggestion dismisses it. That's why there's a cross to the right of the Auto-text suggestion: when you touch it, you close it.

If Auto-text makes a change you don't want, use the Delete key to go back to the end of the word, and a new bubble will appear above the word showing what you originally typed, together with any other suggestions for what you might have been trying to type. Touch one of these options, and your chosen text will replace the Auto-text. The iPad is programmed to learn from you over time so it can improve its suggestions to you.

In the Accessibility settings of your iPad (see Chapter 2), you can set the iPad to speak Auto-text suggestions out loud, even if you don't use VoiceOver. This can be a good way to make sure you notice the suggestions when you're typing quickly or looking at the keyboard. If you can't hear the suggestions, check your iPad's volume is turned up.

## Creating your own shortcuts

If you find you often type the same long word or phrase, you can speed up your typing by entering an abbreviation that the iPad will automatically expand for you every time you use it.

To configure any abbreviations you want to use, go into the Settings app, tap General, tap Keyboard, and then tap Add New Shortcut at the bottom of the screen. In the Phrase box, enter the full phrase you want to abbreviate. In the Shortcut box, type in the short form you want to use. When you type this shortcut in a Note, Message, form box on a website, or email, the iPad will suggest the long phrase using Auto-text and you just need to tap the space bar to accept the suggestion.

To delete any of your Auto-text additions, go into the Settings app, tap General, tap Keyboard, and then tap Edit in the top right. You'll see a list of your shortcuts, with a delete button beside each one (a round red sign with a white bar). Tap the delete button beside the shortcut you'd like to remove and then tap the Delete button that appears on the right to confirm. Tap anywhere else if you change your mind and don't want to delete.

I use a three-letter sequence to stand in for my full email address, so I can quickly enter it when I want to log in to websites.

# Editing your text

Sometimes, you'll want to change what you've written in a note. You might spot a mistake you made when you first typed it, need to update it with new information, or find the iPad's dictation feature has already scrambled the eggs on your shopping list. The editing features of the iPad have some similarities with other computers, but also introduce some new ideas.

## Positioning the insertion point

The insertion point is what Apple calls the cursor, the vertical flashing line that indicates where characters will be added when you type. As with a word processor, when you press the Delete key, characters to the left of the insertion point are removed.

To reposition the insertion point, just tap your note in the place you would like the insertion point to appear, and it will jump to the end of the nearest word.

You can't put the insertion point in the middle of an empty space on the page. If you tap in the space after the last piece of text in your note, the insertion point will go to the end of your text. To create blank space between bits of text, add some blank lines with the Return key.

If you want to move to the middle of a word, tap the word and hold your finger on the screen. You might find it easier to do this accurately if you make the text larger, using the Accessibility options in the Settings app (see Chapter 2).

A magnifying glass appears above the insertion point (see Figure 3.7) to show you where the insertion point is in your word, which gets around the problem of your finger obscuring your view. As you move your finger left or right, the insertion point will move through the word, and you will be able to see it in the magnifying glass. When you remove your finger, the insertion point stays where you moved it using the magnifying glass.

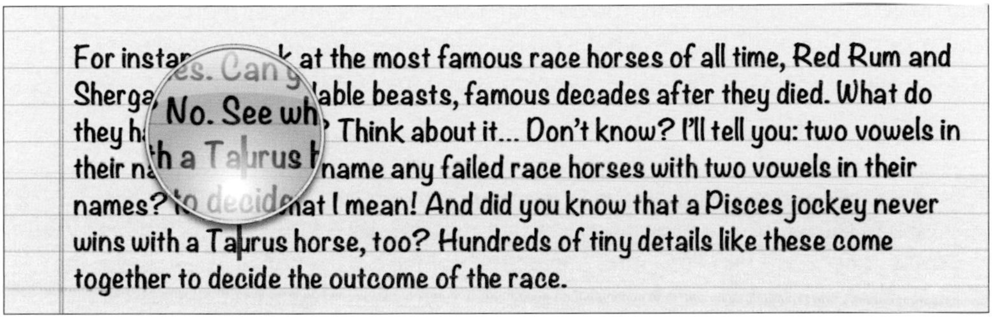

For instan**e**. Can **k** at the most famous race horses of all time, Red Rum and Sherga **No. See wh**lable beasts, famous decades after they died. What do they h **h a Ta**urus hThink about it... Don't know? I'll tell you: two vowels in their n **h a Ta**urus hname any failed race horses with two vowels in their names? **to decide** at I mean! And did you know that a Pisces jockey never wins with a Taurus horse, too? Hundreds of tiny details like these come together to decide the outcome of the race.

**Figure 3.7**

Once you have positioned your insertion point, you can add or delete characters using the keyboard.

## Using cut, copy and paste

Sometimes, you might want to move a chunk of text around, and perhaps even move it from one application to another. You might want to copy something from a web page into a note, for example, or put part of a note into an email you're writing. The Notes app enables you to select chunks of text so that you can move them around within Notes or between different applications.

The first step is to select the piece of text you want to use. There are three ways to do this in the Notes app:

● Tap the insertion point. A menu will appear, with the options Select and Select All. Tap Select, and the nearest word will be selected. Tap Select All, and all the content of the note will be selected.

- Tap and hold your finger on a word anywhere in your note. The magnifying glass appears so you can position your insertion point. When you lift your finger, the menu appears with the options to Select or Select All. Tap Select to select the word, or Select All to select your entire note.

- Double-tap a word to select it.

You can tell what text has been selected because it's highlighted in blue. There's also a menu above it, which we'll come to in a moment. First, take a look at the vertical lines at the start and end of the selected text (see Figure 3.8). Each has a bobble on the end, called a grab point. To increase or decrease the area selected, you touch a grab point and move your finger across the screen. A rectangular magnifier helps you to see what you're selecting. This is how you select a few words, sentences or paragraphs, or even just a few characters.

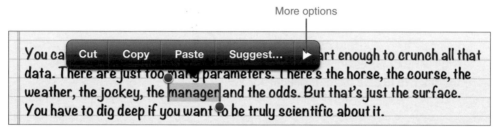

Figure 3.8

Spend a few minutes practising selecting text, including sentences and paragraphs. It doesn't take long to get the hang of it, but it is one of the more fiddly techniques to learn on the iPad.

The menu above your selected text will show you some or all of the following options (Figure 3.8):

- **Cut:** If you cut a piece of text, it will be removed from your note but will be temporarily kept in the iPad's memory. You can then insert your text in a different place in your note, by pasting it there.

- **Copy:** If you copy a piece of text, it will be left where it is now, but a temporary copy of it will be made so that you can paste it (insert it) somewhere else in your note as well.

- **Paste:** If you select some text on screen and then choose Paste, it will delete the text you have selected and paste the last piece of text you cut or copied in its place. You won't need to use this option often.

To select one of the menu options (Cut, Copy or Paste), just tap it. To change your mind and do nothing, tap the selected text or tap somewhere else in the note. When you're moving text around in your note, most of the time you just need to select the text, copy or cut it, move the insertion point where you want to paste it back in, and then tap the insertion point. If some text has been cut or copied, there will be a Paste option you can tap to insert it in your note.

The iPad can only 'remember' one chunk of text at a time, so be careful not to lose anything – take particular care when cutting text. When you cut a piece of text it is removed from your note but kept in the iPad's memory. If you then cut or copy another piece of text before pasting the first one, the iPad forgets your first piece of text and you can't get it back.

If you want to delete a chunk of text, select it in the same way and then tap the Delete key on the keyboard. If you've hidden the keyboard, tap the note to show it again before you select your text. If you select text and then type something, your new text will replace the selected words.

## Fixing your spelling

The iPad will give you a helping hand and fix some of your spelling as you type. You might even find yourself depending on some of its suggestions to speed up your typing. There's no need to tap Shift before the letter 'I' if you're talking about yourself, because the iPad will change the word 'i' to 'I'; and if you type 'ive' it will automatically change it to 'I've'.

The iPad is less confident about correcting other spellings, but if a word isn't in the dictionary it will underline it with red dots (see 'scienc' in the first line in Figure 3.9).

When you tap the word, suggestions for the correct spelling will appear from the dictionary (see 'wil' in Figure 3.9). You can tap one of these suggestions to replace your original word with it.

See, there's an awful lot to the scienc of racing, b    will    ail    wail
close to mastering it. They just pick a name they like the look of, or choose a
horse at random. Like that would ever work! I don't think you wil believe me if I
tell you that of all the people I meet on a day to day basis, only a tiny proportion

**Figure 3.9**

This works when the iPad spots the mistake, but sometimes you'll pick up on mistakes that the iPad won't notice. If you wrote 'Germany', it wouldn't dare question your judgement, even if you should have written 'German'. In that case, you can try some additional options that appear in the menu above selected text:

- **Suggest:** If you select a word and choose Suggest (see Figure 3.8), the spellchecker will suggest alternative words to replace the one you've selected. When you tap one of the suggestions, it will replace the original word with your new selected word. Like a computer spellchecker, this feature can't always correctly identify what you intended to write.

- **Define:** If you're not sure you've used a word correctly, the good news is that the iPad's dictionary is not just a word list. It includes detailed definitions and a mini encyclopaedia. When you tap Define, a bubble opens showing the definition of your selected text. This bubble is quite small, so if the definition is too long to fit in the bubble, drag its text up to read more. If Define is not available as an option, the word isn't in the dictionary.

If there are too many options to fit in the menu above your selected text at the same time, tap the arrows on the right and/or the left of the menu to move between the different sets of options (see Figure 3.8).

Of course, if the correct word isn't in the dictionary, you can correct the mistake yourself in the normal way by repositioning the insertion point and using the keyboard to add or delete characters.

# Adding and deleting notes

When you started Notes for the first time, it opened with a blank note. When you want to write additional notes, you need to tap the Add Note button (the one with the plus sign at the top right, see Figure 3.10). That will open a new blank page, but your previous note will remain in the app for you to refer back to at any time.

You can also delete notes by going to a note and then tapping the bin icon at the bottom of it (Figure 3.10). A red box will appear saying 'Delete Note'. Tap that to get rid of your note, or tap somewhere else to keep your note.

You can browse through your notes using the Previous Note and Next Note icons.

There is no undo for deleting notes, so don't delete something you might regret!

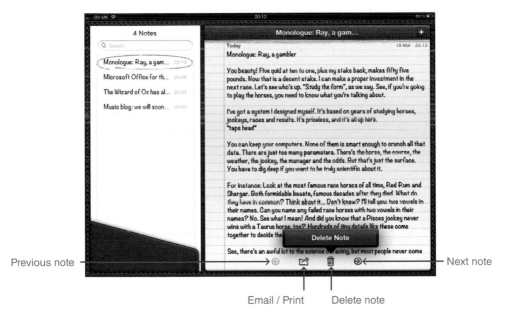

Previous note — Email / Print   Delete note — Next note

**Figure 3.10**

## Emailing and printing notes

At the bottom of each note is an icon that looks like an arrow jumping out of a box (see Figure 3.10), which you can tap to email a note to someone. Chapter 5 shows you how to set up email on your iPad, so that you can use this button to quickly share what you've written.

You can also find the option for printing notes behind this icon. Apple uses a wireless technology it calls AirPrint, which enables your iPad to send documents to a compatible printer without physically connecting to it. If you don't already have an AirPrint-compatible printer, look out for one next time you have to upgrade.

## Searching your notes

I have a stack of wire-bound notebooks and often spend time thumbing through them trying to find something I jotted down weeks or even months ago. The iPad saves you that kind of hassle because it has a search capability built into it. Depending on what you use Notes for, this can be a powerful tool. If you keep recipes in Notes, for example, you could search by ingredient to see what you can concoct from what's left in the fridge. If you're using Notes to keep track of DIY jobs, you could search by room or by tool to help you plan your weekend.

When you're writing notes, think about the kind of words you might want to use to find them later. You could add a few words to the end of a note that you might want to search by, just to make it easy to find the note later.

### Using the search in Notes

The search pane in Notes is shown on the left of the screen in landscape mode, or pops up when you press the Notes button in portrait mode. It lists your most recently updated notes, with the latest at the top of the list, and a snippet showing the first few words to help you to tell them apart. The current note is circled in crayon (see Figure 3.10) and you can choose any of the others by tapping it in the list.

To search your notes, tap the search box at the top of the search pane (see Figure 3.11). You then use the keyboard to enter a word or phrase from the note. It doesn't have to be from the beginning, or even be a complete word. Anything that you can remember from the note can be used to find it again.

List of notes

Search box          Cancel

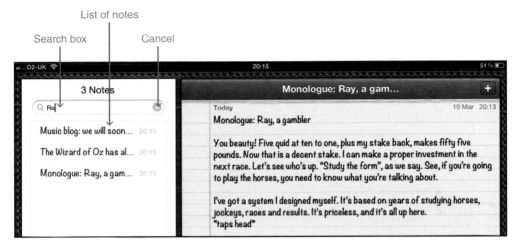

Figure 3.11

As you type, the iPad will search through your notes and narrow the list of notes underneath the search box to those that feature the word or phrase you're looking for. When you've found the note you need, tap it in the list to open it.

While you're typing in the search box, an 'X' in a circle appears in the right of the search box (see Figure 3.11). Tap this to cancel what you've entered. You'll see this feature used in lots of other apps.

## Using the iPad's Spotlight search

There's another way to search Notes and other content on your iPad. The Spotlight search rummages through all the built-in apps to find a note, photo, email or other file that you're looking for. It can also find apps by name, and provides a shortcut for searching the Internet, or for searching the online encyclopaedia Wikipedia.

Wikipedia (www.wikipedia.org) is an encyclopaedia that anyone can help to write. It has more than 3.9 million articles in English, and around 100,000 active contributors. Its coverage of popular culture is much stronger than conventional encyclopaedias, but it has been criticised in the past for some high-profile inaccuracies.

To go to the Spotlight search, press the Home button to return to the Home screen and place your finger somewhere in the middle of the screen. Move your finger quickly to the right, and lift it. This gesture is called a flick. The Spotlight search screen will roll into view from the left. To go back again, you can put your finger in the middle of the search screen (above the keyboard) and flick it to the left. It doesn't matter if you touch an icon when you flick. As long as your finger moves, the iPad will work out that you intended to flick the screen, not tap the icon.

The Spotlight search looks like Figure 3.12. Once you've added songs, films, contacts and more to your iPad, Spotlight will help you to find them all. Until then, it can help you to find notes and apps on the device.

**Figure 3.12**

When the Spotlight search appears, type what you are searching for into the search bar at the top of the screen. As with the search in the Notes app, the search results update as you type. Your notes will appear in the search results with an excerpt from the start of the note. Tap a note extract to go straight to that note. If you can't find what you're looking for, tap the Cancel button in the right-hand corner of the search box to start again.

When you come to install your own apps later, Spotlight can save you a lot of time hunting around to find the icons. If you want to try starting apps using Spotlight, try searching for 'calendar' 'notes', and 'maps'.

> Try moving between the Home screen and the Spotlight search screen using the flick gesture, to practise the technique. The flick gesture is used in many apps, including Notes, to rapidly scroll through content. If you have a long note, try flicking up on it to scroll through it quickly.

As you install your own apps, additional Home screens will be added and you use the flick to move between them too. From the Home screen, flicking right takes you to the search and flicking left takes you to the next Home screen full of apps. If you try flicking left from the Home screen now, you'll see the icons move a little and then bounce back because there isn't another screen of apps to go to.

You can also use the Home button to move between the search screen and the Home screen. If you press the Home button when you're on the Home screen, it will take you to the Spotlight search. If you press the Home button from the search screen, you go back to the Home screen. But where's the fun in that? Buttons are so last century — it's all about gestures now!

## Using the Reminders app

The Notes app is great for capturing lists and ideas, but for notes that have a deadline or date associated with them, there's an even better app. The Reminders app is a simple to-do list manager that ensures you don't forget anything important. To start the app, tap its icon on the Home screen.

> If you don't have the Reminders app on your iPad, see Chapter 2 for advice on upgrading your iPad's software.

The Reminders app looks like Figure 3.13. On the right, there's a page where you can jot down a list of things you need to do. Tap the next blank line on this page and the keyboard appears so you can type in a short description of whatever you need to remember. To add another item, tap the Return key.

**Figure 3.13**

If you want to add extra information to an item, tap the description you've entered for it and a small box will appear on the left. There's a Delete button and a Show More button which enables you to add notes or set a priority. If you want to be reminded when you need to complete this task, tap Remind Me, and then tap the switch for On a Day. Tap the date and time and a box will open with a 'barrel roll' control (see Figure 13.3), which moves a bit like a fruit machine or slot machine. There are 'barrels' for the date, and hour and minutes of the time, and you change them by touching them and moving your finger up or down. You can also flick them to make them move quickly. When you've set the alert time, tap Done. You can set your alerts to repeat, so if you have a task you carry out each day, week, fortnight, month or year, you can enter it once and the iPad will remind you each time it's due.

When you have completed a task, tap the tickbox beside it and it will be removed from your Reminders list. You can switch between viewing your completed and outstanding reminders by tapping Completed or Reminders on the left. If you tick a task as completed by accident, you can find it in the Completed list and tap its tickbox again to return it to its original list.

To browse your tasks by the date they are due, tap Date in the top left to reveal a calendar. Drag it up and down to browse through the months, and tap any day to see the tasks that are due on it. Today's date is marked in red. Tap List in the top left to return to the list view again.

If you want to create new lists for your reminders or delete any of your existing lists, tap Edit in the top left. Tap Create New List and then enter the name of the list to create it. The way you delete a list is similar to the way you delete your Auto-text additions, covered earlier in this chapter.

To change the sound used to alert you to reminders, go into the Settings app and choose Sound. The alert will make a sound when your reminder is due, and will also display a message on your Home screen, so that you notice it when you come back to the iPad even if you're not there when the alert sounds. You can change how your iPad reminds you using the Notification Centre, which is covered in Chapter 7.

## Summary

- Notes is an app that is used for writing, reading and searching text, from shopping lists to stories.

- You can't change the formatting of individual notes, but you can change the appearance of all notes to make the app easier to use.

- You can use Notes in portrait or landscape orientation. The keyboard is bigger if you choose landscape.

- Touch a note to make the keyboard appear.

- You can tap the Shift key and then press a letter to enter a capital letter. Double-tap Shift to switch the caps lock on.

- There are two special keyboards for numbers and symbols.

- If you press and hold on some keys, additional options will appear, such as accented letters.

- You can undo by tapping the Undo button on the numbers keyboard or by shaking the iPad, which is more therapeutic.

- Auto-text tries to predict what you're typing. To accept a suggestion, tap the space bar. To reject it, tap the suggested word on the screen or just type the rest of your word.

- You need an Internet connection and a third generation iPad to use the dictation feature.

- Tap your note to position the insertion point. To position it more precisely, tap and hold until the magnifying glass appears, and then move your finger left or right.

- There are several ways to select your text. Use the grab points to increase or decrease the area selected.

- You can cut, copy and paste text.

- To see suggested spelling corrections, tap a word that's underlined with red dots.

- You can search your notes within the Notes app, or you can use the Spotlight search, which searches all the content on the built-in apps on your iPad.

- The Reminders app is used to keep to-do lists. You can set your iPad to remind you when a particular task is due.

# Brain training

Congratulations — you've mastered your first iPad apps! Before we move on to explore how you can use the iPad for communications, take a moment to try this quick quiz.

**1. To make it easy to find notes again later, it's a good idea to:**

(a) Put a simple title in the first few words of the note

(b) Add a few words to the end of the note, which you might want to search for later

(c) Use as many obscure words as possible

(d) Check your spelling's right, to make sure that any words you search for can be found in the note

**2. To enter quote marks in your note, you can:**

(a) Go to the numbers keyboard

(b) Go to the special symbols keyboard

(c) Tap and hold the full stop key on the letter keyboard

(d) Tap the space bar twice

**3. If Auto-text correctly guesses a word you're typing, you should:**

(a) Tap the suggestion to accept it

(b) Tap the space bar

(c) Keep typing your word

(d) Press Delete

**4. To position the insertion point in the middle of a word:**

(a) Tap the word

(b) Double-tap the word

(c) Tap and hold the word, and then move the insertion point when the magnifying glass appears

(d) Tap the middle of your note

**5. To go to the Spotlight search, you can:**

(a) Go to the Home screen and press the Home button

(b) Tap the search box in the top left of the Notes app

(c) Go to the Home screen and flick right

(d) Go to the Home screen and flick left

## Answers

**Q1** – a, b, and d     **Q2** – a, b, or c     **Q3** – b     **Q4** – c     **Q5** – a and c

# PART II
## Using your iPad for communications

I've just emailed all our friends, to tell them what losers they are for using clunky, old-fashioned laptops and desktops.

# Managing your address book and birthday list

**Equipment needed:** Your iPad and your address book (whether it's on your computer or scrawled in a beaten up old paper notebook).

**Skills needed:** Experience starting apps (see Chapter 3) and using the iPad keyboard (see Chapter 3).

One of the most useful pieces of information you can carry with you is your address book. If you remember a birthday at the last minute and have to write out a card in the shop, or just want to phone a friend for advice or a chat, you'll be pleased to have your addresses and phone numbers at the tip of your fingers.

The iPad comes with an app called Contacts, which is designed to help you manage your address book. It's a simple app, but it's powerful because it's integrated with many other apps. When you're sending email, you can use the details in your address book to save you having to remember or type in somebody's email address, for example, and the Maps app enables you to find directions to and from your friends' houses quickly.

In this chapter, I'll show you how to manage your contacts on your iPad, and how to use the Calendar app to view your friends' birthdays month by month.

# Browsing your contacts

You can copy contacts from your computer or other devices (see Chapter 2), but if you haven't done that, your address book will be empty, so it won't be easy to visualise how it will look when it's finished. Take a look at Figure 4.1, which shows a page from my final address book, to help you get your bearings.

**Figure 4.1**

On the left, you can see the list of contacts, grouped by the initial letter of their last name, which is shown in bold. The contacts are sorted by second name, but shown with their first name first. You can change both the order of sorting and the order in which the first and second names are displayed by going into the Settings app, tapping Mail, Contacts, Calendars and dragging the screen up to reveal the Contacts settings.

If you have organised your contacts in groups using your computer, you can see these groups on your iPad by tapping Groups in the top left of the Contacts app. To see all your contacts, tap Groups again and choose All Contacts. You can also choose to view your contacts from your computer, from your other devices synchronised with iCloud (see Chapter 2), or all your contacts at once. You can't create or edit groups of contacts using the Contacts app, but if you add a new contact while you're looking at a group, the new contact will join that group.

To scroll the list of contacts, put your finger in the middle of it and drag your finger up or down. You can also flick the list to move rapidly, or tap the status bar above the list of contacts to jump to the first contact.

If you touch one of the letters in the alphabetical index on the left, you'll jump to people whose last name begins with that letter. You can also move your finger up and down this index to scroll rapidly through the address book entries.

When you tap somebody's name, their details appear on the right. You can scroll the contact page on the right up and down too, if it won't all fit in at once.

If you tap the Notes area, you can add comments to their details, such as a reminder of where you met them.

To send your contact an instant message (see Chapter 7), tap Send Message. On iPads with cameras, you can tap the FaceTime button on a contact's page to start a video call with them (see Chapter 6). If it's someone you might want to talk to often, tap 'Add to Favourites' so you can find them more easily in the FaceTime app.

To quickly start a new email to a friend, tap their email address. Tap their real-world address to see their home in the Maps app. When the iPad with an integrated teleporter eventually ships, I expect you'll be able to materialise there in a single tap too!

If you want to send a contact's details to somebody else, tap the Share Contact button (see Figure 4.1) at the bottom of the contact's details. You can then choose to share by email (see Chapter 5) or by instant message (see Chapter 7). To remove any information that's out of date, such as an address or phone number, swipe across it to reveal a delete button. If somebody moves house or has other changes in their circumstances, you can update your address book by tapping the Edit button while their details are on screen. The process for editing a contact is similar to the process for adding one, which I'll tell you about next.

## Adding contacts to your iPad

Now you can see how the app is laid out, it's time to add a contact. Start by tapping the Add Contact button. This is marked with a plus sign, and is at the bottom of your list of contacts on the left-hand page of your contacts book (see Figure 4.1).

A new page in the contacts book will open, with a form for you to complete (shown in Figure 4.2). I've hidden the keyboard so that you can see the whole form, but it will open with the keyboard in view at first, so you'll need to scroll up and down to see the full form.

The cursor starts in the box marked 'First', which is for the person's first name. When you've finished filling in a box, either tap Return on the keyboard to advance to the next box down, or tap the box you'd like to go to next. To add an address, tap Add New Address and the form will expand with space for you to enter a street, city, county, postcode and country. Once you've added one address, you can add another if you want to.

If your iPad has cameras, you can choose a ringtone for this person. This will be used to alert you when they request a FaceTime call with you (see Chapter 6). You can also choose a text tone, which is used to let you know when somebody sends you an instant message (see Chapter 7).

It's easy to customise an entry to include all the information you want it to include. If you tap a label beside a box, such as 'Mobile', you can change it to something else, such as 'Home Fax'. You can also use this to change the description of the different addresses belonging to a particular person (to indicate a home or work address, for example). There is a Notes box, which you can fill with any information you like, and you can scroll the form up and tap Add Field at the bottom to create extra boxes that you can label yourself.

**Figure 4.2**

Pay attention when you are typing in details, because the keyboard layout will change depending on what you're entering. The keyboard you're shown prioritises symbols you need most for a particular entry, such as numbers in the mobile box and the @ sign in the email box.

You can ignore any of the boxes that you don't want to use. When you look at somebody's details later, any sections you left empty won't be shown, which minimises the amount of scrolling you need to do to see all the contact's information. Most people don't have their own website (or 'home page'), for example, so you can usually skip that box.

The Contacts app uses some conventions you've seen in other parts of the iPad, including the way you delete something in a form. If you make a mistake and want to clear a box completely, tap the box to select it and then tap the round X button inside it on the right.

You can also delete an entire section from a contact, such as an address, which uses several form boxes. When you are editing a contact, a round red sign with a white bar appears beside any sections you can delete. When you tap it, a new red Delete button appears on the right of the details. Tap that to confirm the deletion, or tap elsewhere on the contact page to change your mind.

If you have a photo of someone on your iPad (see Chapter 11), you can add it to their contact details too. Tap 'add photo' to get started. If your iPad has a camera, you can take a photo of the person (see Chapter 11 for advice on taking photos). Alternatively, you can choose a photo from your iPad. You can drag the photo to centre it and use the pinch gesture (see Chapter 8) to resize it so it best fits the square space available.

When you've finished adding or updating a contact, tap Done in the top right of the contact form. If you want to discard all your changes, tap Cancel in the top left.

To delete all of a contact's information, tap the Delete Contact button, which appears at the bottom of a contact's details when you edit them.

## Adding birthdays and anniversaries

The iPad can help you to keep track of your friends' birthdays. If you add the dates to your address book, you can use the Calendar app to see them organised in a list, or by month or week.

You can add somebody's birthday to their contact details when you're entering them for the first time, or later on by viewing their details and then tapping the Edit button.

To add a birthday, tap 'add field' and then tap 'birthday'. A box will open with a 'barrel roll' control, similar to the one you saw in Chapter 3 for setting reminder times. You can roll the barrels to choose the date, month and year of your friend's birthday.

The iPad's smart enough to know that birthdays happen every year, so I suggest you enter the year your friend was born, if you know it. If you don't, there is an option to choose no year. When you've finished, tap outside the barrel roll to make it go away.

It is possible to add other dates, such as anniversaries, in the Contacts app, but they won't show up on the calendar unless you enter them directly in the Calendar app. To enter another date, tap 'add field' and then tap 'date'. You can change the description of any date by tapping its label.

Once you've added birthdays to your contacts, you can use the Calendar app to browse them by month, by week or in a list. The beauty of it is that once birthdays have been entered in Contacts, the Calendar will show them every year for you automatically. Figure 4.3 shows the month layout for the Calendar app, including my friends' birthdays. You can select a different view using the buttons at the top, and you can choose a different date using the year/month selector at the bottom of the screen.

**Figure 4.3**

You can use the calendar for all kinds of other things, such as reminding you to pay your credit card bill each month, planning holidays or recording when the family will be descending for dinner. To add a new event, tap the Plus button in the bottom right to open the Add Event window. You can enter the date, description, how often the event should repeat (if at all) and an alert to make sure you don't forget about it (see Chapter 7 for advice on managing alerts across all your applications). You can also send invitations to contacts who have email addresses.

# Searching your contacts

To search for somebody in the Contacts app, tap the Search box (see Figure 4.1) and then start to type part of their name. It doesn't matter if you type their first name or surname. As you type, the iPad will filter the list of contacts underneath the search box so that it only shows those that match what you've typed so far. The moment you see the person you're looking for, tap their name to see their contact details.

To cancel the search and show the full list of results again, clear the search box by tapping the round X button inside it on the right.

One limitation with the search is that you can only find somebody by name. You can't search for everyone who lives in a particular town you're visiting, or search by phone number to see who phoned you and didn't leave a message.

The Spotlight search (see Chapter 3) will find your contacts too.

## Summary

- The Contacts app is used to store information about your friends, family and acquaintances.

- The information you enter in Contacts is available to the Mail, Messages, FaceTime and Maps apps.

- To select a contact, scroll through the list of contacts on the left.

- You can use the alphabetical index to speed up scrolling through the list or jump straight to people with a particular initial.

- You can also search by name from within Contacts, or by using the iPad's Spotlight search, or the Maps and Mail apps.

- To add a contact, tap the Add Contact button.

- You can customise each contact page, adding your own boxes of information or changing the labels against the existing ones.

- The keyboard layout changes depending on which box you are filling in.

- You can ignore any boxes you don't want to complete.

- If you have a photo of somebody on your iPad, you can add it to their contact details.

# Brain training

Is your address book under control? Try this short quiz to find out.

**1. The plus sign underneath your contacts list is used to:**

(a) Make new friends

(b) Add a contact

(c) Scroll the contacts list to show more

(d) Tell a friend you're cross with them

**2. When you're entering an email address, you can find the @ sign**

(a) On the symbols keyboard (.?123)

(b) On the extra symbols keyboard (#+=)

(c) On the letters keyboard

(d) On the Home button

**3. A round red sign with a white bar across it is used to:**

(a) Warn you off entering anything in a box

(b) Delete a contact

(c) Delete some of a contact's information

(d) Tell you you're not allowed to call this friend

**4. You can use the Calendar app to:**

(a) See whose birthday is coming up this month

(b) Remind you whose anniversary it is next week

(c) Set an alert to remind you of your dental appointment

(d) Set a monthly reminder to pay the credit card bill

**5. You can use Spotlight search to see:**

(a) Contacts, searched by name

(b) Photos added in the Contacts app

(c) Everyone you know who lives in France

(d) All your friends who are actors

---

## Answers

**Q1** – b     **Q2** – c     **Q3** – c     **Q4** – a, c, and d (b is only true if you've added the anniversary separately in the Calendar app)     **Q5** – a

# Keeping in touch with friends by email

5

**Equipment needed:** An iPad with a connection to the Internet (through Wi-Fi or mobile communications). An email address, if you have one.

**Skills needed:** Experience starting apps (see Chapter 2) and using the iPad keyboard (also Chapter 3). Familiarity with the Contacts app (see Chapter 4) and experience using email on other computers will be helpful but are not essential.

In this chapter, you'll learn how to send email messages to your friends and read their replies. If you've used email on your computer, you'll find it easy to adapt to using the iPad, especially now you're an expert on the iPad keyboard. Before you can start emailing you'll need to set up the email on your iPad, but I will talk you through the steps you need to take.

If you haven't used email before, you're in for a treat! The iPad makes it easy to keep in touch with friends and family by sending them messages they can read on their computers, smartphones, or on their own iPads. With email, messages wait until somebody picks them up so you don't need your friend to be using their computer at the same time as you're writing to them. It's a bit like sending a letter by post: messages are delivered and sit in the email box in the same way that letters sit on the doormat, until somebody comes home to read them. Email is easy to learn, and once you've started using it to keep in touch with your friends, you'll wonder how you ever did without it.

It doesn't matter whether your friends have iPads or not. The emails you send can be read using a computer, mobile phone or any other email-enabled device. You can read the replies on your iPad, whatever device was used to send you the message.

Computer engineer Ray Tomlinson of US technology company Bolt Beranek and Newman invented the use of the @ sign for email addresses in 1971. He is credited as being the first to send email across a network.

## Creating an email account

To get started with email, you'll need to have an 'email account'. Similar to the way that a bank account stores your money, an email account stores your email messages. There are lots of companies that can provide you with an email account, some of them for free.

Having an email account also gives you an email address. This is used to deliver your messages to you, in the same way that your postal address is used to deliver paper mail to you (eventually). If you have an email address already, you already have an email account and don't need to set up a new one, so you can move on to 'Setting up your email account on your iPad'. If you don't already have an email account, or if you want to use a different one on your iPad, you'll need to create one first.

If you don't already have an email address, Apple's iCloud service comes with a free email address you can use. Your email address will be *something*@me.com, where you get to choose what the *something* is. With so many accounts already registered, you might find your preferred email address is already taken, and you'll have to be creative to find one you like.

To create your me.com email address, go into the Settings app (see Chapter 2), tap Mail, Contacts, Calendars and then tap iCloud. Tap the switch beside Mail to turn it on. If you don't already have a me.com email address, tap Create when prompted. Enter your desired email address, and the iPad will tell you if someone's already snaffled that one and ask you to try again if so. It might take a few goes to find something you can use, so stick with it! Your me.com email address cannot be changed once you've chosen it, so check it carefully before confirming it.

Try adding numbers to your email address, using abbreviations for your surname, or picking place names or names related to your hobbies to come up with a memorable email address nobody else has taken yet.

Once you have created your me.com email address, or switched on Mail for iCloud if you already have a me.com address, your iPad is ready to use for email.

When someone else is playing with the iPad, you can read your me.com emails by logging in with your Apple ID on another device at the **www. icloud.com** website.

## Setting up your email account on your iPad

If you already have an email account, you can use it on your iPad too. It's less hassle to use your existing email address than to switch to another email address and make sure everyone you know remembers to use it. To set up your email address, go into the Settings app and then tap Mail, Contacts, Calendars and tap Add Account. You'll see a set of logos showing the different email services you can set up. Although they're colourful, there's no explanation, so this screen can seem a bit unfriendly. The logos are:

- **iCloud:** If you have an email address that ends in me.com, you can choose this option and then log in with your Apple ID to set it up.
- **Microsoft Exchange**: This is mainly used for business email, and it's unlikely you're using it at home. Even if you use other Microsoft software on your computer, including Windows, this is not usually the setting you need.

- **Gmail, Yahoo, AOL, Windows Live Hotmail**: These are called webmail accounts, because the main way people access them is using a website. They're simple to set up, so if you need to create an additional email address for some reason, I recommend choosing one of these services. You can register for a free email address at their websites (**www.gmail.com**, **http://mail.yahoo.com**, **www.aol.com**, and **www.hotmail.com**, respectively).

- **MobileMe**: This was Apple's email service before iCloud was introduced. You only need this option if you have a MobileMe account. (MobileMe is an old service that Apple has replaced with iCloud.)

- **Other**: This covers all other email addresses, including email accounts provided with broadband subscriptions. If you usually store your email on your desktop computer, and you can read it there even when the Internet connection is switched off, this is most likely to be the option you need.

In the following sections, I'll show you how to set up the most common types of email account on your iPad: webmail and the mysterious 'other'.

Your iPad needs to be connected to the Internet so it can check the account details you provide are correct, and so it can download your emails. Make sure you have a Wi-Fi or 4G/3G connection (see Chapter 2) before proceeding.

## Setting up Gmail, Yahoo, AOL and Windows Live Hotmail accounts

The iPad is programmed to recognise email accounts from Gmail, Yahoo Mail, AOL, and Microsoft Live Hotmail, so you don't have to type in much information. Start by tapping the logo of the email account you want to use. Figure 5.1 shows the short form you then need to complete:

- **Name**: Tap this box and then enter your full name here. The iPad will automatically use a capital letter for the first character of each word. This is the name your friends will see on any messages you send them, so they'll know to open them straight away. This option is not shown for Windows Live Hotmail.

- **Address**: Tap this box and enter your full email address here. It will be something like username@gmail.com, username@yahoo.com or username@ aol.com. When you're typing in an email address, the @ sign is on the letters keyboard, towards the bottom right.

- **Password**: Tap this box and then enter the password you use to log in to your webmail. Remember that the characters of the password will appear briefly on screen, so you should set up your email somewhere reasonably private. Once you've set up your email, you won't have to enter your password again.

- **Description**: The iPad will complete this automatically, but you can change it to something else if you prefer by tapping it and typing your description. It's useful only if you're planning to set up lots of email addresses on your iPad.

**Figure 5.1**

When you've finished, tap the Next button at the top right of the form. The iPad will then check that your information has been entered correctly and, if it has, it will give you options to synchronise your calendars and notes, as well as email. They say that a man with a watch knows the time, and a man with two watches is never sure. So if you use the calendar in Yahoo, Windows Live Hotmail, or Gmail, it makes sense to synchronise it with your iPad so that they contain the same information. You can also synchronise contacts and reminders with Yahoo and Windows Live Hotmail.

If you synchronise your notes, you will be able to read them by logging in to your webmail account. If you synchronise more than one email account with your notes, there will be new options for adding notes to your different email accounts in the Notes app. You access these options by tapping Accounts in the top left of the Notes app. When you log on to your webmail in Yahoo and AOL, your notes will be in a folder called Notes. In Gmail, they will have the label of 'Notes'. Unless you can see an immediate use for Notes synchronisation, I wouldn't bother with it.

When you've finished, tap the Save button at the top right of the form, and the iPad will start to download your emails (if you have any).

The default suggested name in an email account on the iPad is John Apple-seed. This is a reference to the legendary Johnny Appleseed (real name John Chapman), who distributed apple seedlings throughout the midwest United States. By the time he died in 1845, he owned 1,200 acres of orchard and had helped to create many more.

## Setting up other email accounts

If you don't have a me.com, Gmail, AOL, Windows Live Hotmail or Yahoo email account, then the option you are most likely to need is called 'other'. This applies if you use an email address provided to you by your broadband supplier, satellite TV company, phone company, or any other company. One of my friends buys her broadband service from her favourite supermarket, and the email address that comes with that falls under 'other' too.

Unfortunately, the 'other' option is much harder to set up than a webmail account, and you might need help from whoever set up your email account on your computer, or from your email provider's technical support.

The first form is similar to the one for webmail accounts (see Figure 5.1), so follow the guidance for webmail accounts to complete it. Your email address will probably look like yourname@yourprovider.com or yourname@yourprovider.co.uk, although you might have full stops, underscores or numbers as part of your address too.

The password is the first technical challenge, because you might not even know your email address has a password. It's usually stored in your email program so you don't have to type it in every time you download email. To find out your password, check any correspondence you have from when you set up your email account originally, or seek technical support from your email provider. If you're calling them, don't dial yet, though. There's a whole lot more they'll probably need to tell you, so read on to see what else you need to know first. If you have a Mac, you can find the password in the Keychain Access utility.

When you have completed the form, you need to tap Next at the top right. The next form (shown in Figure 5.2) carries forward some of the information you've already added but asks for additional information, which you'll need to get from your email provider.

**Figure 5.2**

At the top of the form are two large buttons marked IMAP and POP; these are the two different ways to access email. They work in slightly different ways, which only really matter if you're going to use multiple devices to access your email. If you read your email on POP, any other devices using the same email account won't know when you've read messages or made other changes to them. So you could read your emails on your iPad, but they would still show as new messages when you check your email on your computer. If you read your email messages on your iPad using IMAP, they will already be marked as having been read when you see them on your computer. As a rule of thumb, you can use POP if the iPad will be the only place you read your emails. If you'll be using your iPad and your computer to check your email, choose IMAP. Not all email services support both, so if in doubt, check with your email provider which of them is available to you. Tap the POP or IMAP button to select it, and it will turn blue.

You also need to provide the host name for your incoming and outgoing mail servers. These are all details you'll need to get from your email provider, but they will usually be published on its website. If you go to **www.google.com** and search for 'set up email' plus the name of your email provider, you should be able to find something helpful.

Your incoming mail server will also require a username in addition to the password you've already provided. The outgoing mail server username and password are described as optional – but it's not your choice whether you need to use them or not! If your email provider requires you to use them, it should be able to tell you what these are, but they won't be published on its website.

To scroll the form so you can see the bottom part of it underneath the keyboard, touch the form and then drag your finger up the screen, similar to how you scrolled notes in Chapter 3. The scrolling won't work if you touch outside of the form.

When you've completed the form, tap Save at the top right, and your email will be set up.

You can add multiple email accounts to your iPad by repeating the instructions for setting up an email account above. If you go into the Mail app before setting up an account, you'll be asked to set one up and will be given options like those in the Settings app, described earlier. If you want to add additional addresses or change your settings, you'll need to use the Settings app, though.

# Sending an email

Now it's time to brighten up somebody's day by sending them an email message. As long as you've got a friend's email address to hand, you're ready. If you don't know anybody else's email address you could try sending yourself an email for practice, but don't expect any surprises in the reply.

To get started with email, open the Mail app. It usually sits on a shelf, called the 'dock', at the bottom of the Home screen, but if you've moved it (see Chapter 12), you can find it using the Spotlight search (see Chapter 3).

> To make sure you've noted a friend's email address correctly, check it against this simple guideline: An email address always has exactly one @ sign in it, and at least one full stop after the @ sign.

To start sending an email, tap the New Email icon in the top-right corner of the iPad's screen. It looks like a pen and a piece of blank paper (see Figure 5.3).

New email

**Figure 5.3**

## Addressing your email

When you start to write a new email, a message window opens and a keyboard slides into view, so your screen looks like Figure 5.4.

The cursor starts off in the To box, which is where you enter your friend's email address. Because the iPad knows you're entering an email address, it gives you a keyboard that's designed to make that easy. The letters keyboard is enhanced with the @ sign, hyphen and underscore characters (see Figure 5.4), so you can type them without having to switch to the symbols keyboard. If the email address has numbers in it, tap .?123 to open the numbers keyboard, as you did when typing notes in Chapter 3. When you finish typing an address, tap the Return key, and a rounded box will appear around the email address.

Pick from contacts

Delete

@ sign
Underscore
Hyphen

**Figure 5.4**

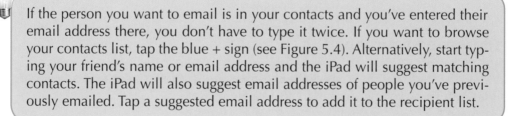

If the person you want to email is in your contacts and you've entered their email address there, you don't have to type it twice. If you want to browse your contacts list, tap the blue + sign (see Figure 5.4). Alternatively, start typing your friend's name or email address and the iPad will suggest matching contacts. The iPad will also suggest email addresses of people you've previously emailed. Tap a suggested email address to add it to the recipient list.

It's possible to send the same message to several people at the same time, so after you've entered an email address your cursor will stay in the To box so that you can add any additional email addresses there, either by typing them or by selecting them from your contacts.

As well as adding multiple recipients in the To box, there are two other ways you can address an email to somebody:

● **Cc**: This sends someone a courtesy copy of the email. This is often used when you want to keep someone informed about the conversation you're having but you don't expect them to get involved in replying. Everyone who gets a copy of the email can see the email address of everyone who has been sent the message using To or Cc.

● **Bcc**: This works like Cc except that the B stands for 'blind', so nobody else can see that this recipient has received a copy of the email. Those who receive a Bcc copy can still see the To and the Cc recipients, though. If several people receive a Bcc copy, they can't see each other's email address either. You can use this if you're emailing people who don't know each other and who might not want you to give out their email addresses to each other.

If you want to use Cc or Bcc to address somebody, tap the Cc/Bcc box and separate rows will open for Cc and Bcc. You can then tap these and enter the email addresses or contacts into them.

If you need to delete an email address from the email, tap that name or email address and then tap the Delete key on the keyboard (see Figure 5.4).

When you finish completing a box, you can tap Return to advance to the next box. If you want to Cc or Bcc someone, you'll have to tap the Cc/Bcc box, though, because tapping Return in the To box will skip over it and take you straight to the email subject.

## Writing your email message

Once you've addressed your email, you can craft your message. There are two parts to this: the subject line and the message itself.

The subject line of the email is a short description of what it's about. It helps people to tell different email conversations apart and find messages they need more easily. In most email programs, the first thing people will see is your name and the email subject, and they'll have to open the email to see the rest. It's a good idea to have a clear, concise and meaningful description that will uniquely identify your message. Something like 'Planning August theatre outing' is much more useful than 'Chat', and emails with blank subject lines can be easily overlooked. On the iPad, the subject line is positioned between the addressees and the main message area, in common with other email programs you might have used.

Underneath the subject box is a large box in which you write your email message. You write your message in the same way you write notes (see Chapter 3), and the keyboard reverts to the same layout as in the Notes app. The Auto-text, selection, copy, cut, paste and editing features all work in the same way as they do in Notes. You can copy and paste pictures as well as text in emails, though, for example, if you find one on a website you want to share.

When you select text and tap the insertion point (see Chapter 3), there are some formatting options you don't have in Notes. If you tap BIU, you can choose from bold, italic and underlined formatting. There's also an option for Quote Level formatting. You don't need to use it, but you'll probably come across it in the menus at some stage. It's used to indent a piece of text to indicate that it's a quote from an earlier email. When you've finished composing your message, tap the Send button at the top right of the email form. If you have an Internet connection, your message is immediately sent to the recipient. Otherwise, you'll see an error message, but your email will be stored on your iPad and sent next time you open the Mail app and do have an Internet connection.

If you decide to abandon the email, tap Cancel at the top left. You'll have the option to save a draft of the email, which means it won't be sent but will be kept in your draft folder so you can edit and send it later. If you delete the draft, the email will be permanently deleted.

Cheekily, Apple puts a line at the end of each message that says, "Sent from my iPad" to make sure all your friends think about buying one too. This is the email 'signature', which concludes every message you send. You can change it to something else if you prefer, such as your full name and favourite quotation. To edit this, go into the Settings app, tap Mail, Contacts, Calendars and then tap Signature.

Email works a bit differently on the iPad to the way it works on a computer, so it might take a few minutes to get the hang of it. Once you have, though, you can send messages from anywhere you take your iPad and have an Internet connection. Give it a go!

# Reading your emails

After you've sent out a few messages, hopefully you'll get a few replies. If your iPad is set up with the same email account as your desktop computer, you might already have a stream of messages flowing in.

The Mail app probably looks a bit different to the email programs you've used before, so it might be hard to see at a glance how you do things like read an email, reply to one or delete one you don't need any more.

When you go into the Mail app, it will download your latest emails, and you'll see a screen like the one shown in Figure 5.5, if you're using your iPad in landscape orientation. If you rotate your iPad, you'll see just one email at a time, but you can swipe from the left of the screen to show the message list, and can swipe it back the other way to hide it again. The portrait orientation is useful if you're reading long emails, but the landscape format stops you having to tap so often to open new messages, so I'll stick to that in this chapter.

The column on the left shows a list of the messages in your inbox, with the most recent at the top. You can scroll the message list up and down by putting your finger on it and dragging it up or down, or by flicking it. To jump back to the top, tap the status bar above the list (see Figure 5.5).

The number in brackets at the top of the list of messages tells you how many unread messages you have in your inbox.

**Figure 5.5**

Each email has a summary box in the message list detailing who sent it, the time (today) or date (before today) the email was sent, the subject line, and a short snippet from the start of the message. Unread emails have a blue bobble beside them, so you can quickly identify them. When you tap the email's summary box, the email's entry in the message list is coloured blue and the full email opens on the right and can be scrolled up and down in the usual way. Figure 5.5 shows my welcome email from iCloud on the right.

If the email is part of an ongoing conversation, its entry in the message list will include a number in a grey box to indicate how many messages there are in that conversation, or 'thread' (see the first email in Figure 5.5, which is part of a thread with two messages). When you tap the email in the message list, the list will change to show only the previous emails you've received with the same subject line. To see all your messages again, just tap the Inbox button in the top left.

If the iPad spots an address, phone number, email address or link, it underlines it in blue. Touch and hold the underlined text for options, including showing places on a map and adding details to contacts. Tap a location to see it on a map or a website link to visit it.

There are several things you can do with an email once you've selected it in the message list (see Figure 5.5):

● **Add the sender as a contact**: Tap the sender's name and you can create a new contact for them, or add their email address to an existing contact. Because you can choose email recipients from your contacts list, this can make it easier to send emails to that person in future.

● **Reply to or forward the email**: Tap the arrow in the top right, and you can choose to reply to the email or forward it to somebody else. After that, the process is similar to writing a new email. If you reply to a message, a curved left arrow appears beside it in the message list. If you forward a message, a right-pointing arrow appears.

● **Print**: If you have a compatible printer, tap the arrow in the top right to find the print option.

● **Delete/Archive email**: Tap the dustbin icon in the top right and the email you're reading will be moved to the Trash folder. If you have a Gmail address, the dustbin icon is changed to an arrow pointing to an archive box. When you tap the archive box icon, your email is archived, which means it vanishes from your inbox but is still available if you need it later (in the All Mail folder).

● **Mark as unread or flag**: If you read a message but want to leave it marked as unread, tap Details at the top right of the message, then tap Mark. You can then mark it as unread, or put a flag beside it in the message list as a reminder to yourself that you need to do something with it.

● **See all the recipients**: Tap Details at the top, to see who else got a copy of the email.

- **View an attachment**: Scroll to the end of an email message to see any attachments it has. Tap the attachment and it will open. Tap and hold the attachment if you have more than one app that can open it and you want to choose which app to use. When you've finished, tap Done in the top left. If necessary, tap the document first to make the Done button appear. The iPad can also play audio or video attachments. Touch and hold a photo or video to save it in your Camera Roll album on your iPad (see Chapter 11).

> You can also delete an email by swiping left or right over its entry in the message list and then tapping the Delete button that appears in the message list. If you don't want to delete, tap elsewhere in the message list.

## Managing email folders

So far, everything you've seen has taken place in the Inbox, the folder where new emails are filed. There are other mailboxes you can use, which include:

- **Drafts**: If you abandon an email halfway through writing it but save it so you can finish and send later, this is where you'll find it.

- **Sent**: This folder stores the emails you have sent to others.

- **Trash**: This folder contains emails you have deleted. You can empty the Trash folder by going into it, tapping Edit and then tapping Delete All.

- **Archive:** This folder, where available, is there to store old emails.

- **Bulk Mail, Junk or Spam**: Where offered, this folder contains email that your email provider believes is junk email. It's worth checking this folder from time to time in case your email provider has moved a real message to this mailbox by mistake.

To access all of your folders, tap Mailboxes in the top left of the screen (see Figure 5.5). You can then choose a folder from the list, which might look similar to Figure 5.6. If you have multiple email accounts, the Mailboxes button will instead show the name of your account. You can tap this to see all your folders, and then tap Mailboxes to see a list of your email accounts to choose from. Choose All Inboxes to see all your incoming emails from different accounts in the same place.

Edit button

**Figure 5.6**

To create new folders on your iPad, view the mailboxes for an email account (so you see a folder list like Figure 5.6, including Inbox and Sent) and then tap the Edit button (indicated in Figure 5.6). You can then tap the New Mailbox button at the bottom to create a new folder, so you can file away emails relating to particular people or activities. While you're editing your mailboxes, you can delete or rename some of them by tapping their names. The iPad won't let you meddle with the Inbox, Drafts, Sent Mail and other essentials, though. When you've finished editing your mailboxes, tap Done at the top of the column.

When you're reading an email, you can move it into a different folder by tapping the Move button (indicated in Figure 5.5) and then choosing a folder.

To move or delete lots of messages in one go, tap the Edit button at the top of the message list. Then tap the messages you'd like to select, and tap Delete or Move at the bottom of the column. If you're moving messages, tap the folder you'd like to move them to. Tap Cancel at the top of the message list if you change your mind.

# Searching your emails

You can use the Spotlight search to find emails, or you can use the search function built into Mail. Whichever you use, it can only search for people an email was received from or sent to, or the subject line. That's another reason good subject lines are important.

The search built into Mail works in a similar way to the one in Notes (see Figure 5.7). You go into the appropriate mailbox, tap the Search box at the top left, and then type the name or word you're looking for. Matching emails appear underneath and you can tap any of them to read them. To cancel the search, tap the Cancel button (see Figure 5.7). To clear the search box and start looking for something else, tap the X in the circle in the search box (see Figure 5.7).

**Figure 5.7**

# Downloading new emails

Your email messages are stored in a mailbox managed by your email provider. Your iPad then downloads these emails to its internal storage over the Internet. It starts by downloading the most recent 50 emails (you can change this number in the Settings app) and then you can tap Load More Messages at the bottom of the message list to download another batch.

Whenever you go into the Mail app, your iPad checks for any new email messages in your mailbox. At any time you like, you can make it check for more new messages by tapping the Update Mailbox button at the bottom of the message list (indicated in Figure 5.5).

Some types of email account (including iCloud) can automatically push new messages to your iPad shortly after they arrive in your mailbox, as long as you have an Internet connection. This means you get messages almost as soon as they're available, but the drawback is that it runs down your battery more quickly.

For accounts that can't push messages to you, the iPad can automatically check at regular intervals (15, 30 or 60 minutes) to see whether you've had any new messages. Again, this is something that will run down your battery more quickly, and it isn't necessary if you won't be checking what's been downloaded for some time anyway.

By default, the iPad is set to allow emails to be pushed to your iPad where possible, but it doesn't have regular checking activated. You can change these settings by going into the Settings app and tapping Mail, Contacts, Calendars. If you want to conserve battery power, you can turn off automatic pushing of messages and regular checking.

If you tire of the pinging and whooshing noises, go into the General settings to switch off the sounds you hear whenever you send or receive an email.

The Mail icon on the Home screen has a red circle in the corner of it showing how many unread messages you have in your main inbox. You can customise how the iPad tells you about new messages, as you'll learn in Chapter 7.

## Summary

- You can use the iPad to read emails sent using any kind of device or computer. Emails from your iPad can be read using any email-compatible device, too.

- The Mail app is used for reading and writing emails.

- The easiest way to set up email is to use the free iCloud email account.

- The most common webmail accounts can be quickly set up by entering your email address and password.

- Use the Other option to set up most other types of email account, including those typically provided by broadband suppliers.

- You can pick people from your contacts to send an email to.

- To send someone a copy of an email, use Cc. To send someone a copy of an email but hide their details from everyone else receiving it, use Bcc.

- Use a clear and specific subject line.

- To add the same text to the end of all your outgoing messages, such as your full name, edit the email signature in your Settings app.

- The message list shows a short preview of the messages in your mailbox. Tap one to read it in full.

- A threaded email is one that is part of a discussion. Tap it in the message list to see the previous emails with the same subject line.

- Tap the curved arrow in the top right to reply to an email, forward it or print it.

- When you receive an email, you can add its sender to your contacts so it's easier to email them in future.

- You can move emails between different folders.

- The search will find emails by sender name, recipient or subject line.

- Some types of email account can push emails to your iPad when they arrive. Your iPad can also check for emails regularly. To save battery power, turn off the automatic updating of email.

# Brain training

At the end of that bumper project, relax with a short quiz to see how much you've remembered.

**1. Which of these is a valid email address?**

(a) fred@example@com

(b) www.example.com

(c) fred.bloggs@examplecom

(d) freddieboy@example.com

**2. To set up a Gmail account on your iPad, you need to know:**

(a) Your username

(b) Your incoming and outgoing server details

(c) Your password

(d) Whether it is IMAP or POP

**3. A good subject line might be:**

(a) Stuff

(b) Hello

(c) Thought you'd like this

(d) Booking tickets to see The Australian Pink Floyd

**4. An email thread is:**

(a) A group of sent messages

(b) An email message that's as long as a piece of string

(c) A group of emails with the same subject line

(d) A folder of messages

**5. To find a party invitation email in your inbox, search using:**

(a) The name of someone else who got a copy of the invitation

(b) The name of the pub mentioned in the message

(c) The word 'birthday', which was in the subject line

(d) The name of the person who sent you the message

## Answers

**Q1 – d**      **Q2 – a and c**      **Q3 – d**      **Q4 – c**      **Q5 – a, c and d**

# Using FaceTime for video calls

6

**Equipment needed:** An iPad with built-in cameras and a Wi-Fi connection. A friend with a FaceTime-compatible device and the FaceTime app.

**Skills needed:** Familiarity with the Contacts app (see Chapter 4) is helpful.

If you have a first generation iPad, which doesn't have built-in cameras, then I'm afraid you can't use FaceTime. Skip ahead to the next chapter!

When Apple launched the second generation of the iPad (known as the iPad 2), it added video calling. For many years, technology like this – the ability to see who you're phoning as you speak to them – was the stuff of science fiction. In recent years you might have used a webcam with your computer to have a video chat with people over the Internet, but that meant you only ever got to see people sitting in front of their computers. The iPad, with its two built-in cameras, makes this kind of technology much more portable, so you can chat to people from all over your house as well as many other places.

You can't chat just anywhere, though: even if you have a 4G/3G-compatible iPad, a Wi-Fi connection needs to be available for you to be able to use the video-calling feature. As you know, these are often provided in cafés and holiday resorts, so it's usually easy to get connected for a chat. The upside of using Wi-Fi is that it's usually free, which, oddly, makes video calls cheaper than many phone calls.

The app used for video calling is FaceTime, and the iPad comes with this already installed on it. The person you want to talk to must also have FaceTime, but they don't necessarily need to have an iPad; they may have FaceTime if they have an iPhone, an iPod touch or an Apple Mac computer, as FaceTime software is also available for these. Not all versions of these devices support FaceTime, but if the device has a camera on the front, it should work with FaceTime. FaceTime comes preinstalled on mobile devices and new Macs and is sold separately for older Macs.

FaceTime is a fantastic feature of the iPad. It's strange, but after a video chat you really do feel like you've met someone. It feels completely different to a phone call.

Tap the FaceTime app on your Home screen to get started.

If you don't have the FaceTime app on your Home screen, your iPad might not be compatible with it. Remember, you need an iPad with built-in cameras for FaceTime to work. If you do have a compatible iPad, check you haven't disabled FaceTime in the Restrictions settings (see Chapter 2).

## Logging in to FaceTime

To use FaceTime, you need to log in using your Apple ID. This is the same email address and password combination you used when you set up your iPad, and which you'll use to download music and video (see Chapter 9) and apps (see Chapter 12) from the App Store. If you don't have an Apple ID, tap the Create New Account button.

If a friend wants to set up a FaceTime call with you, they'll need to use your email address. The FaceTime app will ask you which email address you want people to use to contact you. If you're happy to use the same email address as you use for your Apple ID, just tap Next in the top right. Otherwise, tap the email address itself and you can delete it and type in a new address. Tap Next when you've finished.

You can also add additional email addresses for yourself in the FaceTime section of the Settings app. This is useful if you have multiple email addresses and friends might try to contact you using any of them.

When you enter an email address for FaceTime, you might need to verify it is yours. If so, Apple will send you an email with a link in it. You'll need to check your email using your computer and click the link Apple sends you. This proves to Apple that you own the email address, and acts as a security measure for Face-Time because it stops people from using email addresses they don't own. You won't need to verify your email address if the email address you enter is already linked to your Apple ID or is one that you have already set up in the Mail app (see Chapter 5).

You can leave your iPad signed in to FaceTime so that you don't have to enter your email address and password the next time you want to use it. If you want to log out for some reason (perhaps to enable someone else to use FaceTime with their own ID), you can do that by going into the Settings app, tapping FaceTime on the left and then tapping your Apple ID.

## Starting a FaceTime call

The first shock you get when you start the FaceTime app is that you see your own face filling the screen (see Figure 6.1). That's me, by the way. Nice to meet you.

Down the right hand side of the screen is a list of people to call. If you tap Recents at the bottom, you can see people you've recently called, tried to call or received calls from. The Favourites section shows you people you've labelled as 'favourites' within FaceTime or the Contacts app. Tap Contacts to see people in your address book, which is shared with the Contacts and Mail apps. This is a great time saver, because it means you don't have to enter a friend's email address again if you've already done so in Contacts or Mail. You can tap Groups at the top of your con-tacts list to access different groups of contacts.

If you haven't added the person you want to talk to as a contact in your iPad, you need to do that before you can call them. FaceTime makes it easy to add a contact by tapping the Add Contact button (the plus sign) in the top right corner of the screen (see Figure 6.1). As a bare minimum, you should add their first name, last name and the email address or iPhone phone number they use for FaceTime. You don't need to enter any further details to use FaceTime but, if you wish, you can flesh out your contact's profile with more detail so it's there for you to refer to in the Contacts app. For advice on completing your contact's details, and a refresher on how the Contacts app works on the iPad, see Chapter 4.

**Figure 6.1**

To find the contact you want to call, you can scroll the contacts list by touching it and dragging your finger up and down, or you can use the search box at the top of the screen. Tap somebody's name and you will see full contact details for them. This provides you with three particularly useful options:

- **Add to favourites**: Since not everyone in your address book will have FaceTime, you can save yourself a lot of time by adding those who do have it to your Favourites list. You can then see a list of only these people by tapping Favourites at the bottom of the screen.

- **Edit**: To make a FaceTime call to your friend, you will need to contact them using the email address or phone number they have registered with Apple for use in FaceTime. That might not be the same address they use for correspondence, so, if necessary, you'll need to tap the Edit button in the top right and add their FaceTime email address or phone number to their contact details.

- **Start a FaceTime call**: There's no big button to press! To start a FaceTime call, just tap the email address your friend uses for FaceTime, or their iPhone phone number.

When you tap an email address or phone number, FaceTime will attempt to call your friend and you'll hear a simulated phone ringing sound. Your friend will see a message on screen and hear an alert sound if they have alerts enabled. When your friend answers, you'll see their face on the screen.

If the iPad tells you almost immediately that someone you're trying to call isn't available for FaceTime, it's probably because FaceTime doesn't know that email address. Check you've got the right email address and that you've spelled it correctly.

## Talking to a friend with FaceTime

During a call, the FaceTime screen looks like Figure 6.2. Most of the screen is filled with the video of your friend, but overlaid on this are a few controls as well.

In the top left is a small picture showing what your friend is seeing of you. If this is in the way of something you want to see in your friend's video, you can touch it and drag it to another corner of the screen, but you can't get rid of it. Most of the time, you can just leave it alone. It's worth keeping an eye on this from time to time to make sure that you're not covering the camera with your thumb, or giving your friend an unflattering view up your nostrils. The camera on the front of your iPad is opposite the Home button, so it's best to hold the iPad near its corners or to stand it up to avoid blocking the camera.

Mute      End call      Swap cameras

Image courtesy of Kim Gilmour

**Figure 6.2**

At the bottom of the screen are three buttons. On the left is a Mute button, which is probably more acceptable in business than personal use. It seems a bit rude to stop someone you've called from hearing what you're saying, but if you need a moment of privacy, this button will give you it. The images continue, however, so don't rely on the Mute button if your friend can lip-read!

On the right is a button to swap between using the cameras on the front and back of your iPad. Most of the time, you'll want to use the front-facing camera, so that you can see your friend on the screen and they can see you looking at them on the screen. Sometimes you might want to share something that's going on, however, such as the view from your window, or a birthday party. Tap the Swap Cameras button, and FaceTime will use the camera on the back of your iPad instead of the front. That means your friend will be able to see whatever you point your iPad at, and you'll still be able to see what they're seeing and their reaction to it on your screen. The back camera is in a corner near the Sleep/Wake button – take care with how you hold your iPad when using the back camera, to make sure you don't cover the lens. To revert to using the front-facing camera, simply tap the Swap Cameras button again.

If you want to move around as you talk, try not to move too quickly. The image can become blocky and indistinct if you move too fast, so it's best to prop your iPad up on the desk if you're just chatting, or move the iPad around slowly if you're giving your friend a tour.

Remember that you need a good Wi-Fi connection to use FaceTime. If you move too far away from the Wi-Fi hotspot while you're chatting, your connection might break up, resulting in poor quality sound and video.

If you rotate your iPad, the view on the other person's screen will also rotate, so that your friend always sees things the right way up.

You can break off the video chat to look something up on your iPad while you're still talking. You could look up someone's address in the Contacts app, for example, if you're arranging to meet at their house later. Press the Home button and you will go to the Home screen, where you can start another app. The video your friend sees will be paused, and your own screen will be filled with the Home screen and whatever apps you use, so you won't see any video either. You can still hear and speak to each other, though. When you're ready to go back into FaceTime, tap the green bar at the top of the screen where the iPad says 'Touch to resume FaceTime'.

When it's time to finish the call, tap the End Call button in the middle of the screen at the bottom.

After you've had a successful call with someone, a video camera icon also appears beside their email address or phone number when you view their contact details in the FaceTime app, which is a helpful reminder of which one they use for Face-Time when you want to talk to them again in future.

# Receiving a FaceTime call

Your friends can request FaceTime chats with you too. If your iPad has been muted (see Chapter 2), you won't hear anything, but otherwise you will hear your iPad make an alert sound. If you've specified a ringtone for your friend in the Contacts app (see Chapter 4), your iPad will use that sound to let you know who's calling. You'll also see a message telling you who would like to have a FaceTime chat with you. There are two buttons: Decline, which will block the call; and Accept, which will start the call straight away. If your iPad is locked when the FaceTime call is requested, there is just a single control available: a slider to start the call. If you've just stepped out of the shower and are in no state for video calling, you can ignore it, or press the Sleep/Wake button to put your iPad to sleep again.

If you don't want to be interrupted by FaceTime requests, you can turn FaceTime off in the Settings app.

## Summary

- The FaceTime app enables you to have video calls with friends.

- It is available for the iPad, iPhone, iPod touch and Mac computers (but not for the first generation of the iPad, which does not have built-in cameras).

- To use FaceTime, you need to have a Wi-Fi connection.

- You log in to FaceTime using your Apple ID.

- People contact you using the email address you have entered in FaceTime.

- You need to add someone to your contacts before you can call them.

- To start a call, tap someone's email address or iPhone phone number in the FaceTime app.

- You can swap between the front or back camera when using FaceTime.

- If someone wants to have a call with you, you'll see a message on your iPad's screen.

- In the Settings app, you can turn off FaceTime or add additional email addresses that people can use to contact you.

# Brain Training

How did you get on with FaceTime? Find out with this quick quiz.

**1. You can use FaceTime to call some- one with:**

(a) A third generation iPad

(b) A first generation iPad

(c) A Windows PC

(d) An Apple Mac computer

**2. People contact you on FaceTime using:**

(a) Your iPad's serial number

(b) Your phone number

(c) Any email address you have

(d) Any email address you've entered in FaceTime

**3. To use FaceTime on your iPad, you need to have:**

(a) An iPad with cameras

(b) A 3G Internet connection

(c) A Wi-Fi Internet connection

(d) A Mac computer

**4. To turn off the video but keep the audio working in a FaceTime chat, you:**

(a) Tap the Mute button

(b) Press the Home button

(c) Tap the Swap Cameras button

(d) Tap the End Call button

**5. To make sure your FaceTime calls go well, you should:**

(a) Check you're calling the right email address or iPhone number

(b) Keep your fingers away from the camera lens

(c) Make sure your iPad is not muted so you hear the ringtone

(d) Comb your hair

## Answers

**Q1** – a and d     **Q2** – d     **Q3** – a and c     **Q4** – b     **Q5** – a, b, c and d

# Sending instant messages using iMessage

**Equipment needed:** An iPad and an Internet connection.

**Skills needed:** Experience with using the iPad, including gesture controls, using the keyboard, and starting and using apps. Familiarity with the Contacts app (see Chapter 4) is helpful.

In the previous chapter, you learned how to video conference with friends using FaceTime. In this chapter, you'll learn about a way you can chat with friends that's a bit more socially acceptable if you're still in your pyjamas.

The Messages app provides a convenient way to send text messages and photos to friends who also have an Apple device with the Messages app, such as a Mac (after Summer 2012), an iPad, an iPhone or an iPod touch. Because the messages all go through Apple's network, you don't have to pay to send or receive messages if you use Wi-Fi. Even if you don't have Wi-Fi available, Apple doesn't charge you for sending or receiving messages, but you might have to use some of your mobile data subscription to exchange messages. This is different from standard mobile phone text messages (SMS), which are typically charged individually or included as part of a subscription package. The iPad's large keyboard makes it much easier to type messages than it is on a mobile phone, too.

The Messages app was introduced with Apple's iPad software update in October 2011 and it was important enough that Apple made it the first app on the Home screen. If you don't have the Messages app on your iPad, see Chapter 2 for advice on updating your iPad software.

To send and receive messages, you need to have an Internet connection. To get started, tap the Messages icon on your Home screen.

The first time you use Messages, you need to sign in with your Apple ID. This is the same email address and password combination you use for FaceTime, to buy content from iTunes or the App Store, and for other services on your iPad.

The app is called Messages, but when you get into the app, you'll see the service is called iMessage.

## Sending messages

Figure 7.1 shows the Messages app with a conversation in progress. If you've used the Mail app on your iPad (see Chapter 5), the screen layout will feel familiar. Your conversations are listed on the left and you can tap one to read it in the panel on the right or to pick up the conversation where you left off. You can scroll the conversation by touching the messages area on the right and dragging it up or down.

Here's how to send a message:

1. To start, tap the New Message button (see Figure 7.1).

2. In the To box, enter the email address your friend uses for their Apple ID, or the number of their iPhone. You can also just type someone's name to select them from your Contacts. If the person you enter is not registered with iMessage, their details will be highlighted with a red alert. Tap the details to remove them and try another email address or phone number.

3. Tap the message box (with rounded corners) above your keyboard and type your message (see Figure 7.1). You can use the dictation feature where available (see Chapter 3) if you prefer.

4. To add a photo or video, tap the camera button to the left of the message box. You can pick an existing one from your iPad, or take a new one using the iPad's cameras.

5. Tap the Send button beside the message box when you've finished.

**Figure 7.1**

Your messages are shown on the right of the screen in blue speech bubbles, and your friends' messages to you are shown on the left in grey speech bubbles (see Figure 7.1).

When your message has been read, the word 'Delivered' appears underneath it if the recipient has enabled this feature. If delivery fails and your friend has enabled read receipts, you'll see a warning to that effect and you can tap it to try sending again. If you'd like your friends to see when you've read their messages, go into the Settings app and tap Messages, and then flick the switch to allow your iPad to send read receipts.

If you want to delete parts of a message or forward parts of it to someone, tap the Forward/delete button in the top right (indicated in Figure 7.1). Tap which pieces of the conversation you want to forward or delete and then tap either the Delete or the Forward button at the bottom of the screen. If you choose to forward a message, enter the recipient's email address or phone number at the top and then tap Send next to your message.

You can send a message to several people at once. Just enter all their email addresses or iPhone numbers into the To box.

If you'd like to send someone a smile, you can use the Emoji keyboard, which has pictures representing a wide range of emotions (see Figure 7.2). First, you need to enable this special keyboard. Go into the Settings and tap General on the left, and then tap Keyboard. Tap International Keyboards and then tap to add a new keyboard. Among all the different keyboards (including French and Spanish), you'll find the Emoji one. Tap its name, and when you go back into the Messages app, you'll see a globe key beside the space bar. That key takes you to the Emoji keyboard, and back to the normal keyboard again when you've finished. You can swipe left and right across the faces on the Emoji keyboard to see more symbols, and tap the keys at the bottom with pictures on them to reveal new sets of symbols, including a jolly Santa, musical instruments and world flags. Tap a picture to add it to your message. This is a fun feature, especially for surprising friends who haven't worked out how to do it yet!

Return to letters keyboard

Recently used symbols    Switch between picture sets

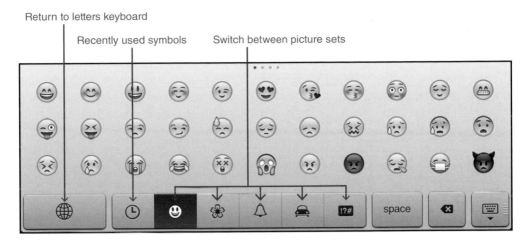

**Figure 7.2**

# Splitting and centring the keyboard

You can make it easier to hold the iPad and type messages on it at the same time by splitting the keyboard into two halves. Each half of the keyboard shrinks so that you can rest the iPad in your fingers and reach all the keys on the screen with your thumbs. You can also move the keyboard from the bottom of the screen to the middle, so it's easier to rest the iPad in your hands while typing

To find these options, tap and hold the Hide Keyboard key (see Figure 7.1), and then tap Split or Undock (which moves the keyboard up). To return the keyboard to its normal form, tap and hold the Hide Keyboard key to find the options to Dock and Merge.

These options are perhaps most useful in the Messages app, but you can use them in any other app too, including Mail, Contacts and Notes.

You can also split the keyboard by putting two fingers on it and moving them apart horizontally. Reverse the gesture to merge the keyboard again.

# Managing message alerts through the Notification Centre

If you're not using the Messages app when a message comes in for you, you can choose how the iPad alerts you. You can do that by changing your notification settings, which give you control over how apps get your attention when they have new information or messages for you. That means you can decide how intrusive you will allow each app to be. In the case of Messages, you might let the app interrupt whatever you're doing with an alert because there's a friend waiting for your reply.

To set up your notification settings, go into the Settings app and tap Notifications on the left. On the right, you see a list of your applications. Tap an app's name, and you'll see its notification settings. These look like Figure 7.3, which shows my settings for the Messages app.

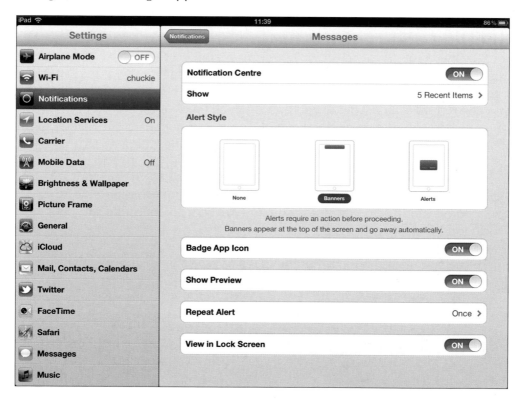

**Figure 7.3**

You have several options for notifications. First, you can choose whether you want them to appear in the Notification Centre. This is a panel that shows you notifications from across different applications (see Figure 7.4). You can see the panel when you're using any app or Home screen. Just touch the status bar (or put your finger above the touch screen area) and pull your finger down the screen to pull the panel into view. If you tap an item in the Notification Centre, you can go straight into the appropriate app for more information or to take action. To stop an application from clogging up your Notification Centre, you can limit the number of recent items that appear there.

**Figure 7.4**

You can also choose to receive an alert or a banner when an app has new information for you. An alert pops up in the middle of the screen and won't disappear until you do something with it, such as tapping a button to make it go away. A banner appears at the top of the screen briefly and then disappears of its own accord. If you want neither of these options, you can choose None instead.

Some apps can also change the app's icon, for example by putting a number on it to show you how many unread messages you have (as the Messages icon in Figure 7.4 shows). Switch the Badge App Icon on to enable this feature where available.

For the Messages and Mail apps, you can also choose to show a preview of the message with the alert (this is recommended). The Messages app can also repeat the alert up to 10 times if you miss it the first time, although I'd avoid using that if you often leave your iPad near other people. They could find it annoying to be stuck in a room with an unattended iPad that keeps chirruping.

If you enable notifications to appear in the Lock Screen, you'll see a box in the middle of the screen showing the update when you return to your iPad. You can unlock your iPad and go straight into the app associated with the update by touching the app's icon (see Figure 7.5) in the notification box and dragging it to the right.

App icon

**Figure 7.5**

If you want to know who's sent you a message without even looking at the screen, you can give them a distinctive alert sound. In the Contacts app, select the name of the person and tap Edit to change the text tone which is used to tell you about a new message. There's a great selection of quirky noises provided with the iPad and you can buy additional tones in the iTunes store (see Chapter 9), including classic lines from movies and snippets of hit songs.

To change or disable the sounds associated with different alerts, go into the Settings app, tap General on the left and then tap Sounds.

# Summary

- The Messages app enables you to send instant messages, photos and videos to friends who also have the app.

- You can use a Wi-Fi or 4G/3G connection.

- Your conversations are listed on the left, and you tap one to enter it on the right.

- Your messages are shown in blue speech bubbles on the right, and your friends' are shown in grey bubbles on the left.

- You can address a message to someone using their email address or iPhone number. You can pick someone from your contacts by typing their name.

- You can choose a photo or video from your iPad or use your iPad's cameras to create one.

- To make it easier to hold the iPad and type, you can split the keyboard and move it towards the middle of the screen.

- The Notification Centre gives you updates from across your apps in one place.

- You can also choose to see an alert or a banner when there is a new message for you.

# Brain training

Let's finish up, as usual, with a short quiz.

**1. When you've finished writing your message, you should:**

(a) Tap Return on the keyboard

(b) Tap the Send button

(c) Tap the New Message button

(d) Tap the Hide Keyboard button

**2. If you swipe from the status bar down the screen:**

(a) You return to the Home screen

(b) You reveal the Notification Centre

(c) You go to another open app

(d) You can crop a photo

**3. If you put your fingers on the keyboard and move them apart horizontally:**

(a) You'll zoom in on the message

(b) You'll move the keyboard to the centre of the screen

(c) You'll split the keyboard

(d) You'll type some strange meaningless characters

**4. If you want to see how many messages you have waiting for you on the Home screen:**

(a) Turn on alerts for the Messages app

(b) Turn on banners for the Messages app

(c) Turn on the Notification Centre for the Messages app

(d) Turn on Badge App Icon for the Messages app

**5. To customise the sound played when Kieran sends a message:**

(a) Change the ringtone associated with him

(b) Change the sounds in the Settings app

(c) Change the text tone associated with him

(d) Go into the iTunes store

## Answers

**Q1** – b          **Q2** – b          **Q3** – c          **Q4** – d          **Q5** – c

# Browsing the web on your iPad

**Equipment needed:** An iPad with an Internet connection (Wi-Fi or 3G).

**Skills needed:** Experience of editing text and using the iPad keyboard (see Chapter 3).

One of the best features of the iPad is the ease with which you can browse the Internet. From the comfort of your sofa, a café, or even in bed, you can look at family photos on Facebook, book your holiday, do your banking or search for the answer to pretty much any question. Almost everything you can do online with a conventional computer, you can do with the iPad.

I said *almost* anything. One thing the iPad doesn't support is Flash, which is a format used for playing animations, music and video on the Internet. Nobody will mourn the loss of those irritating splat-the-monkey adverts you sometimes see on websites, but if you like to play games online, you might find some of them don't work on the iPad. Video sharing website YouTube still works (see Chapter 10) but you won't be able to play the video and audio on some websites. For most people, the lack of Flash isn't a real problem, though.

To get started, make sure you have a web connection (see Chapter 2). The app you use for viewing web pages on the iPad (known as the 'web browser') is called Safari. You can find it on the Dock at the bottom of your Home screen, on the left.

If you are using a 3G/4G connection, don't worry about how long you're connected. It's not like a phone call where you're charged by the minute. You only pay for the content you download, so it's the amount of content you need to be aware of, not the amount of time you spend on it. It doesn't matter how long you spend reading a web page before going to another one.

In this chapter, I'll show you how to get the most from Safari. You'll build on the skills you acquired in using the keyboard and editing text in Chapter 3, and on your experience of using the Internet on other computers. If you don't already know how to use the Internet, you can read a free chapter from *Social Networking for the Older and Wiser* at **www.sean.co.uk** for a quick introduction.

Start the Safari app, and we're ready to go!

There is small risk that somebody could intercept data you send over the Internet when you're using public Wi-Fi, so it's best to avoid online shopping, banking or other sensitive activities when you're using Wi-Fi in public places like cafés or hotels.

## Entering a website address

The Safari browser looks much like a browser on a desktop computer, so there will be few surprises when the Safari app starts. At the top, you'll see two boxes: one for the website address, and the other for searching the web (see Figure 8.1).

To go straight to a particular website, you need to tell the browser its website address. This usually starts with 'www.' followed by a word or phrase, followed by a domain extension such as .com, .co.uk or .org. Website addresses you've probably used before include **www.bbc.co.uk** and **www.google.com**. These short addresses take you to the website's home page, which is designed to welcome new visitors.

Bookmarks bar    Address field    Clear address field    Search field

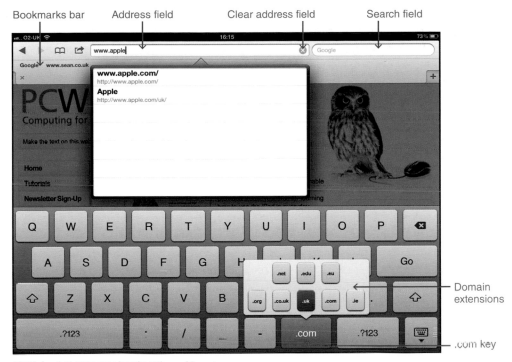

Domain extensions

.com key

PC Wisdom is © 2000-2011 by John Wiley and Sons, Inc

**Figure 8.1**

Every different page of content on the website has its own, longer website address too. You could type the longer address in to jump straight to a particular article on a website, but it's usually easier to go to the website's home page and then click some links to find what you want, or to use the search engine to go there.

To enter a website address on the iPad, start by tapping the address field at the top of the screen (see Figure 8.1). The keyboard will appear so that you can type in the website address.

It is often fine if you leave out the 'www.' at the start, as this is often automatically inserted, so you can save time by just typing in 'bbc.co.uk', for example.

If you mistype anything in the address field, you can edit what you've typed. Tap and hold in the address field, and the magnifying glass will appear so you can easily position your insertion point. You can then type missing letters or use the keyboard's Delete key to remove characters. You can also paste a website address, if you've copied it from an email or the Notes app, for example. Before you paste a new website address into the address field, clear the old one by tapping the Clear Address Field button (the X) in the right of the address field (see Figure 8.1).

When you've finished typing your website address, tap the Go key, which is where the Return key normally is on the right of the keyboard.

While a page is loading, a cross icon is shown inside the address field on the right. Tap this to stop a page loading. After a page has loaded, there is a refresh icon here which you can tap to load the page again.

There are a couple of features that are designed to make it easier to enter website addresses. Firstly, when you're typing in a website address, the keyboard includes the symbols you're most likely to need, and incorporates a .com key. You can use that key to add .com to the end of your address, or another popular domain extension (such as .net, .edu, .eu, .org, .co.uk, .uk or .ie). To add .com, just tap the key normally. To add one of the others, tap the .com key and hold it. A bubble will appear showing those other domain extensions (see Figure 8.1). When it does, slide your finger over to the domain extension you want and then release your finger. This works similar to the way you chose accented letters in the Notes app (see Chapter 3).

The additional domain extensions in the bubble include both .co.uk and .uk. Most of the time, you probably need to choose .co.uk but .uk is the one that's highlighted initially. Make sure you pick the right one!

The other way that Safari helps you to enter websites is that it will suggest websites you might like to visit while you type. These suggestions are drawn from sites you've previously visited, or those you have bookmarked (see later in this chapter). The suggestions appear underneath the address field, as you can see in Figure 8.1.

Each suggestion has the title of the page in bold, with its full website address underneath in grey. If you're returning to a website, keep an eye on these suggestions. The moment the iPad offers the correct suggestion, you can tap it to go there straight away.

## Using the Search box

You can also find websites by using the search field on the right. While you type, Google will suggest phrases that match what you're typing. If one of them is what you want, you can stop typing and just tap it. If not, when you've finished typing, tap the Search key on the keyboard. You'll find it in place of the Return key.

The search feature also enables you to find words or phrases within a web page you're viewing. Above the keyboard is a Find on Page box (see Figure 8.2). Tap this and then type the word you want to search for. As you type, Safari will look for your search term on the page and jump to the first occurrence, highlighting it in yellow. You can move to the next time the word or phrase appears by using the Next button, and can go back to the one before by tapping the Previous button. When you've finished searching in the page, tap the Done button above the keyboard on the left. If you want to see more of the web page while you search it, you can tap the Hide Keyboard button. The Find on Page controls will still be there at the bottom of the screen.

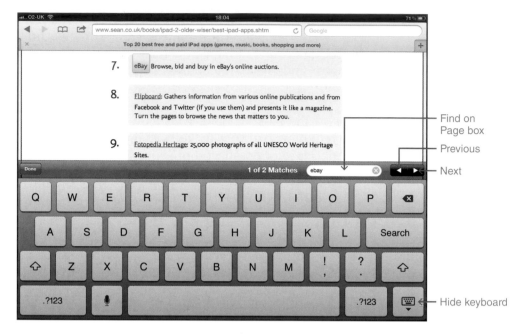

Find on Page box

Previous

Next

Hide keyboard

Figure 8.2

# Zooming the page

Many websites were designed for much bigger screens than the iPad, or use text that is too small to read comfortably. In Chapter 2, you learned about a way you can use the accessibility settings to zoom the whole screen. This feature is ideal for people who have impaired vision, because it enables them to enlarge the iPad's onscreen buttons as well as the content. There is a drawback, in that it sometimes moves the controls off the screen, so you might have to do more scrolling around to find them again.

If you just want to see part of a web page more clearly, the zoom accessibility controls are excessive, so you have a choice of two alternative ways you can enlarge just the content of a web page. Perhaps the simplest is to double-tap a column of text, and it will be enlarged to fill the width of the screen. Double-tap again, and the screen will zoom out again so you can pick another column of text to zoom in on.

There's also a gesture used for zooming, called the pinch. It works like this: you put two fingers on the screen, near the content you want to enlarge (see Figure 8.3). You then move those fingers apart, and the screen will zoom in on the space between your fingers (see Figure 8.4). People usually use the pointing finger and thumb of the same hand, but if this is uncomfortable for you, you can use two fingers from different hands.

*PC Wisdom is © 2000-2011 by John Wiley and Sons, Inc*

**Figure 8.3**

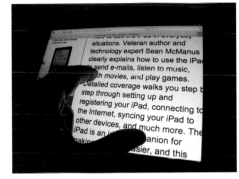

*PC Wisdom is © 2000-2011 by John Wiley and Sons, Inc*

**Figure 8.4**

The pinch is also used for enlarging photos (see Chapter 11). Practise it and you'll find it gives you a lot of control over what you see on your iPad screen.

Pictures can become indistinct when zoomed in too far, but the text of a web page will sharpen when you remove your fingers from the screen.

To go back to the web page's original size, perform the pinch in reverse. Start with your fingers apart on the screen, and then bring them close together. If you shrink the page too far, it will snap back to fit the screen when you release your fingers.

## Scrolling the page

A web page will often spill off the available screen area, especially when you zoom in.

To scroll the page so you can see a different part of it, put your finger anywhere on it and then drag it across the iPad's screen. As you move your finger up or down the screen, the web page will scroll in that direction. If the web page is wide or has been zoomed in, you can also scroll sideways.

While you are scrolling, a thin scrollbar appears at the right and/or bottom of the screen to give you a visual clue of which part of the page you're looking at. The longer the line, the more of the page's total height or width you're looking at. The position of the line also tells you where you are on the page.

For example, Figure 8.5 shows a page I've zoomed in, which has two scrollbars. The one at the bottom shows me that I'm looking at about 80% of the page's width, and I'm looking at the right side. The scrollbar along the right side of the screen shows me that I'm looking at only about 10% of the page's height, and I'm roughly halfway down the page.

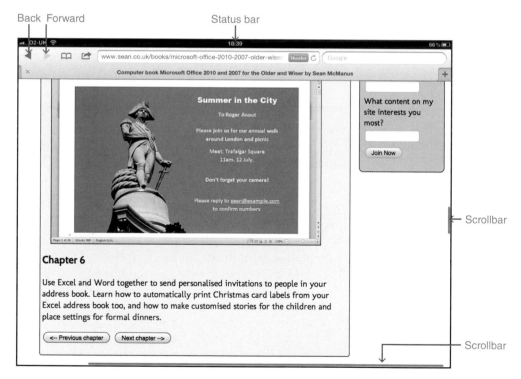

**Figure 8.5**

On a Windows computer, you might be used to seeing a scrollbar at the side of the screen all the time to tell you if there's more to see. You don't get that on the iPad, so it's a good idea to try scrolling the page to see what you might be missing.

You can use the flick gesture you learned in Chapter 3 to quickly move in any direction on the web page, but it's particularly useful for zipping through pages that are several screenfuls deep.

The navigation options for a website are usually at the top of the screen. When you finish reading a page, you can jump to the top of it by tapping the status bar, indicated in Figure 8.5, so that you can find its links.

You can often see more of a web page by rotating the iPad. Try the landscape and portrait orientations to see which you find most comfortable for reading.

## Using links on websites

Now that you know how to view a website, it's time to look at how you can interact with it. As you probably know from your experience with desktop computers, web pages are connected together using links. Links can be text, in which case they are usually underlined, or they can be pictures, in which case they might look like buttons.

To use a link on a website, whether it's text or an image, you just tap it. With all the pinching and scrolling going on, you might think there's a danger of touching the wrong part of the screen and being taken away to a page you didn't want. That doesn't happen: the iPad doesn't decide you've tapped a link until you remove your finger again; if you've moved your finger in between, it guesses you intended to scroll. If you put two or more fingers on the screen at once, it won't select a link for either of them, because you can't choose more than one link at the same time.

Web pages on the iPad look the same as they do on a desktop computer, but there's one significant difference. On a PC, your mouse cursor can be over a link without you clicking it, and this is sometimes used to make a menu appear on the screen. On the iPad, your finger is either touching the screen or it isn't. On a well designed website it should still be obvious where the links are, but you might have to tap first to open menus that normally pop up automatically when you're using a desktop computer.

Like a desktop browser, your iPad is able to take you back to the previous page you looked at, or forward again after you've gone back. The Back and Forward buttons are in the top left of the browser, as indicated in Figure 8.5.

# Entering information into websites

Often you'll want to enter information into a website, such as your username and password, or perhaps your address if you are shopping online. The way you enter information into a website is similar to the way that you added information in the Settings app or addressed emails, but there are a couple of things to look out for.

As you might expect, you tap a text entry box to bring up a keyboard so you can type something into it. The first thing to look out for is that the keyboard layout can change depending on what you're typing in. Some websites tell the iPad you're entering an email address so that you get a keyboard with an @ sign within easy reach, for example, but not all websites do this.

The second thing to look out for is that the Return key on the keyboard is replaced with a Go key. Previously, you used the Return key to move to the next box that you need to complete but here, tapping the Go key submits your form as if you'd tapped the Submit button for the form. If you tap the Go key before you've finished filling in all the boxes, you might have to go back to the beginning and complete the form all over again.

To enter information into other boxes on the web page, therefore, tap the next box rather than tapping the Go key. While the keyboard is in view, you can still scroll the underlying web page to make sure you can complete all the information you need to.

To select a radio button (a radio button is a round one that is used to choose one of several options), tick a checkbox or choose from a pulldown menu, just tap it. In the case of a pulldown menu, the menu will open so that you can tap your option.

## Browsing multiple websites at the same time in tabs

Safari enables you to have up to nine web pages open at the same time. This can be useful when you're shopping online and comparing the offers from different websites, if you're trying to coordinate flight bookings in one window with hotel reservations in another, or even if you just want to take a short deviation and read something such as an encyclopaedia article before continuing to read a news report.

The Safari browser on the iPad uses tabbed browsing, which means you can quickly switch between different web pages you have open at the same time. At the top of the web page is a row of tabs, which show the titles of the web pages you have open. You tap a tab to see its page. Figure 8.6 shows the tabs at the top of the browser.

Tabbed browsing was introduced to older iPads with a software update that was released in October 2011. If you don't see tabs on your iPad, see Chapter 2 for guidance on updating the software on your iPad.

Sometimes when you click a link, it will open in a new tab of its own accord, but you can choose to open a new tab and then use the address field or search box to put a new website into it. To open a new tab, tap the small tab with a plus sign on it on the right of the screen.

The tabs resize depending on how many you have open, so they always fill the width of the screen.

To close a web page, tap the X on the left of its tab. If you're not already viewing that web page, you'll need to tap its tab first.

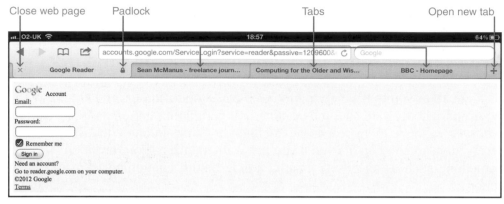

Google screenshot courtesy of Google

**Figure 8.6**

If you're entering sensitive information into the website, such as credit card details, make sure you're using a secure web page. To check, look at the web page title in its tab. A secure web page has a tiny padlock icon to the right of the page title (see Figure 8.6). Don't be tricked by any padlocks in the web page content. If it's not inside the tab, it doesn't count.

When you tap a link, it will usually open in the same tab, but you can choose to open it in a different tab. To do that, tap and hold the link and a menu will appear (see Figure 8.7).

At the top of this menu, you can see the website address the link goes to. You can open this menu if you're not sure about where a link will take you and you want to check its destination before you follow it.

146

The menu's options are:

- **Open**: Tap this option to open the link in the current tab (that is, to replace the page that is open with the new one). This is the same thing that happens if you just tap the link, but it gives you a chance to check where it will go first.

- **Open in New Tab**: Tap this option to open the link in a new tab.

- **Add to Reading List:** Tap this to add the linked page to the Reading List. The reading list is used to keep a record of web pages you plan to read but don't have time to read right now. There's more about the Reading List later in this chapter.

- **Copy**: Tap this option to copy the link's website address. If you want to send somebody the link, you could use this to take a copy of its address and then paste it into an email in the Mail app. There's an easier way to send somebody a link, though, which I'll show you later.

- **Do nothing**: This isn't actually an option on the menu, but if you tap outside the menu, it will close again. That's good to know if you open the menu by accident.

The tabbed browsing feature in Safari can be extremely useful, but you need to take care with it. If you use all nine tabs and then tap a link that opens in a new tab, you'll lose the contents of one of your previous tabs. That doesn't matter so much if you were just reading a website, but if you had started to write something in Facebook or were midway through ordering a new fridge freezer, it might be annoying.

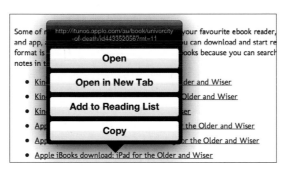

**Figure 8.7**

If a page is taking a long time to download, you can try reading another page in a different tab while you wait.

## Managing bookmarks, history and web clips

If you find a website you want to remember, you can bookmark it. This stores a link to the website in your browser so you can easily find it again.

The idea of bookmarking websites isn't limited to the iPad, and you've probably come across it on your computer. If so, you can synchronise your computer's bookmarks with your iPad (see Chapter 2).

### Visiting websites using bookmarks

Your iPad comes with a handful of bookmarks on it already, including one that takes you to the iPad User Guide. There are two ways you can visit a website that's in your bookmarks.

The first is to use the address field. As you type into it, your browser will check your bookmarks to see if any of them match what you're typing. If they do, it will suggest those websites, so that you can just tap the website's name to visit it. This happens automatically whenever you're using the address field. Start typing 'bbc. co.uk', for example, and you'll see any pages on the BBC site you've bookmarked, which could be the news section or sites dedicated to your favourite shows.

You don't have to type an address into the address field to find a bookmark; you can also type words that are in your bookmark title. Try typing 'user' into the address field, and you'll see the iPad User Guide link appears, even though its actual address doesn't include the word 'user'.

The other way you can visit websites you have bookmarked is to browse your bookmarks. If you don't have a particular website in mind and just fancy meandering through some of your favourite websites, this is the best approach.

To open your bookmarks, tap the Bookmarks button, which has an icon like a book (indicated in Figure 8.8). A menu will open, showing your bookmarks, including any you synchronised from your desktop computer. Each bookmark has a book icon beside it (see Figure 8.8) and you can tap the name or the icon to visit the website.

If you have lots of bookmarks, you can scroll the menu by dragging it.

As you can see in Figure 8.8, Safari already has three special folders of bookmarks set up on it.

- **Reading List:** As I mentioned briefly earlier, the Reading List is used to keep a note of web pages you want to read later. If you just want to see the pages you haven't read yet, tap the folder name and then Unread at the top of the folder's contents. Bear in mind, though, that when you visit a page from your Reading List the iPad assumes you've read it and removes it from the Unread list, even if you got bored after a few seconds and went in search of tea and biscuits instead.

- **History**: This stores links to the websites you've visited recently. You can't add your own bookmarks to this folder, but you can tap the History folder and then tap Clear History to delete this record. As you saw at the start of this chapter, the history is used to suggest websites when you're typing into the address field, so it makes it easier to visit sites you've been to before.

- **Bookmarks Bar**: The bookmarks bar appears underneath the address field when you're using it (see Figure 8.1 at the start of this chapter). This is a good place to keep your favourite websites. To visit one of them, tap the address field to make the bookmarks bar appear, and then tap the name of the bookmark. Your bookmarks bar will be empty at first, but I'll show you how to add websites to it shortly.

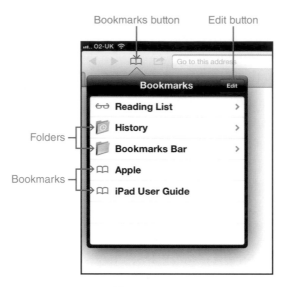

Bookmarks button    Edit button

Folders

Bookmarks

**Figure 8.8**

# Adding bookmarks

The first step in adding a bookmark is to visit the website you'd like to add in the usual way. To bookmark the web page you're viewing, tap the Bookmark/share button – the icon that shows an arrow coming out of a box, indicated in Figure 8.9. When you tap it, a menu opens showing several options, including:

● **Add Bookmark**: Tap this to add a bookmark, using the options shown in Figure 8.9. The name of the bookmark will be taken from the title of the web page, and some will make more sense than others. You can change the bookmark name to be anything you like. You can use the editing controls you've seen in the Mail and Notes apps: tap and hold to make the magnifying glass appear so you can reposition the insertion point for editing; and tap the X button in the title box to clear it. Underneath the bookmark name, you can see the folder it will appear in, which is usually Bookmarks. That means it will go into your bookmarks collection without being filed in a folder. If you want to put the bookmark in a folder you've created, tap the folder box and then choose which folder you want to put your new bookmark in. Note that you need to create a folder (see later in this chapter) before you can add a bookmark to it. You can also add the bookmark to the bookmarks bar. When you've finished, tap Save.

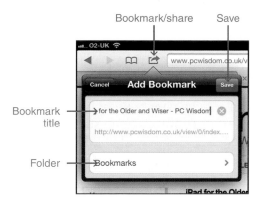

Bookmark/share    Save

Bookmark title

Folder

**Figure 8.9**

- **Add to Reading List:** Reading List pages aren't suggested when you type into the address field and the iPad separates out unread content in the folder, so the Reading List is best used for keeping a temporary note of a particular article you want to read once. As well as your bookmarks, your Reading List can be synchronised with other devices (see Chapter 2), so you could add something to your Reading List on your computer and read it on your iPad later (or vice versa).

- **Add to Home Screen**: If you tap this option, the web page you're viewing will be given an icon on your Home screen, like an app. This is called a 'web clip'. You'll be prompted to enter a name to go underneath the icon, but you only have about 10–15 characters, depending on how wide they are, otherwise your iPad will abbreviate the name to the first few and last few letters. Some websites provide icons designed especially for web clips, but the iPad will use a tiny picture of the web page if no icon is provided. When you tap the icon on the Home screen, Safari will open and take you straight to that web page. I recommend you add your favourite web pages to the Home screen. In Chapter 12, you'll learn how to organise and delete icons on your Home screen, including web clips.

Whatever you type in the bookmark's title can be used to find it in the address bar. So feel free to add any words to the end of your bookmark titles that might make the bookmarks easier to find later.

## Organising your bookmarks in folders

Are you one of those people who spends more on stationery than on bread, or are you happy to throw your paperwork into a big box and hope you never need to find a gas bill at the bottom of it? Well, if you're an organised type, you'll be pleased to know you can arrange your browser bookmarks in folders. If you're not, feel free to skip this bit. You can always jump straight to a bookmark by typing in part of its name or address in Safari's address field. Organised bookmarks are much easier to browse, though.

> If you synchronise with the bookmarks on your computer, they'll arrive on your iPad in the folders they were in on your computer.

You need to create a folder before you can add a bookmark to it. To create additional folders, tap the Bookmark/share button and then tap the Edit button (shown in Figure 8.8). A new menu then appears, with a New Folder option in the top-left (shown in Figure 8.10). When you tap that, you're asked to enter a title for the new folder. There's only room for a few words here, so keep it short and put the important words at the start.

It's possible to have folders inside folders, so underneath the folder title, the iPad shows you which folder your new folder will appear in. Usually this just says Bookmarks, which means you'll see your folder as soon as you open your bookmarks. You can leave this setting alone, but if you tap it, you can pick one of your other folders to put this new folder inside.

When you've finished setting up your new folder, tap the Bookmarks button in the top left of the menu, or tap Done on the keyboard.

When you're in the edit mode, you can change the order of your folders. Put your finger on the Arrange icon (three short lines) to the right of the folder name and without removing your finger, move it up or down the list to change where that folder appears. The folder will stay where your finger is when you lift it from the iPad. This same technique can be used to rearrange the order of your bookmarks, but you can't change the order of Apple's default bookmarks and folders.

New folder

Arrange

Remove

**Figure 8.10**

# Deleting bookmarks

You can also delete bookmarks or folders, except for Apple's default ones. When you edit a folder of bookmarks, red buttons will appear beside those items you can remove, shown in Figure 8.10. Tap one of these buttons, and a red button marked 'Delete' appears to the right of the item. Tap the Delete button to confirm, and your folder or bookmark is gone.

You can also swipe your finger left or right across a bookmark to make a Delete button appear when you're browsing your bookmarks. You don't have to tap the Edit button first if you do that, so it's a bit quicker.

When you're creating or deleting folders or bookmarks, don't tap the Edit button until you're looking at the folder or bookmarks you want to change. If you want to delete a bookmark that's in another folder, for example, tap that folder name first to show the bookmark, and then tap Edit so you can delete it.

## Sharing website content

The web is all about sharing information, and you'll often come across information or pictures online that you want your friends to enjoy too. Safari has several features that make it easy to share website content.

Firstly, you can copy text or a mixture of text and images from a web page using one of the techniques you use in Notes or Mail. Tap and hold your finger on text near the content you want to copy, and the magnifying glass will appear. When you lift your finger, you can select the area you want to copy by moving the grab points, as you learned in Chapter 3. When you tap Copy, the text, images and their layout will be kept in the iPad's memory. You can then go into your Mail app, or other compatible apps, and use Paste to put the content into a new message or other document. For this technique to work, it's important that you tap and hold on ordinary text, and not on a link or image, otherwise a menu will appear instead of the magnifying glass.

Sometimes you can select a whole section of a web page by tapping and holding that section.

If you only want to copy a picture, tap and hold it. You'll be given the option to copy the picture so that you can paste it into an email or other document, or save it. If you save the picture, it will be stored with all your other photos on your iPad. In Chapter 11, you'll learn how to use the Photos app to view the pictures on your iPad.

In Chapter 2, you learned how to change your iPad's wallpaper to one of the photos on your iPad. Now you've learned how to save photos from websites on your iPad. Why not find a great image online and use the Settings app to make it your iPad wallpaper?

There are three further options when you tap the Bookmark/share icon in Safari:

- **Mail Link to this Page**: Tap this and an email box will open, with a new email already started. In the body of the email will be a link to the current web page and the subject line will be the web page's title. Sending a link has the advantage that whoever you're mailing can go straight to the website you want them to see, but it might not mean much to them without some context so it's worth writing a few words to explain what's on the website and why you're sending it to them. You can send an email in this way without leaving the Safari app, so you can carry on browsing where you left off after sending your message.

- **Tweet**: Twitter is a social networking site that enables you to share short messages with friends and strangers online. If you're a Twitter user, you can enter your Twitter account in the Settings app and then use it to post messages and photos from within the Camera, Photos, Maps, Safari and YouTube apps. Each message on Twitter is called a "tweet". When you tap the Bookmark/share button and then tap Tweet, you're given a box to enter a message to go with your web page link. When you tap the Send button, your message is posted on Twitter.

- **Print**: If you have an iPad-compatible printer, you can tap this to print the page. This option feels like the odd one out in this menu to me, because the others are all about keeping and sharing links to the web page. But if you imagine you're printing it for a friend, it's easy to remember where to find the Print button.

You can look up words and phrases in websites using the built-in dictionary too. This feature works the same as in Notes, so see Chapter 3 for a refresher.

## Using Reader to make it easier to read pages

Some websites are packed with adverts and have designs that clash so horribly it's hard to concentrate on the content. The Reader feature in Safari attempts to streamline a web page so that you only see the article you want to read, without any of the adverts or other clutter. If you're reading an article that's split across multiple web pages, Reader can also collect the whole article for you so you don't have to keep following links to the next page. It does sometimes filter out useful content, though, such as videos and comments, and it's not available for every web page.

To use this feature, where available, tap the Reader button in the address field (see Figure 8.11). A plain box will open with the stripped down page content in. You can drag the content up and down and tap links in the usual way. Tap outside the box to close the Reader view.

Figure 8.11

# Using Private Browsing mode

Don't spoil the surprise! If you've used the iPad to book a romantic getaway or order flowers, you might be rumbled if your partner sees the websites you've visited. This could easily happen because the history of websites you've visited is used to suggest websites when someone types into the address field.

To remove the history of websites you've visited, go into your Settings app and tap Safari. You can then clear the history (of visited websites), and the cookies (small files websites use to recognise you when you return) and data (files from websites stored on your iPad to speed up return visits). You can also clear the history by tapping the bookmarks icon in Safari and then tapping the History folder.

To stop your iPad keeping any records of your visits, go into the Settings app, tap Safari and then switch Private Browsing on. When you are in the Private Browsing mode, the top of the browser changes from a silvery-grey to a charcoal colour. You can turn Private Browsing off again in the Settings app when you've finished shopping.

# Summary

- Your iPad's web browser app is called Safari.

- When you are entering a website address, a .com key appears on the keyboard to help you.

- Tap and hold the .com key to use other extensions, including .co.uk.

- Tap and hold in the address field or in a text entry box to reposition the insertion point, copy or paste.

- Your browser keeps a record of the sites you visit to speed up return visits, but you can delete this record or use Private Browsing mode.

- To zoom, double-tap a column or use the pinch gesture.

- You can drag or flick the page to scroll through it.

- To visit a link, tap it. To open it in a new tab, tap and hold it.

- You can have up to nine web pages open at once.

- You can bookmark websites you want to revisit, or add a web clip, which puts an icon for the website on your Home screen.

- To find a bookmark, you can type part of its title into the address field.

- You can organise your bookmarks in folders.

- Bookmarks in the Bookmarks Bar folder are shown when you tap the address field.

- To copy text or a mixture of text and pictures, tap and hold on some text. To copy just a picture, tap and hold the picture.

- To save a picture, tap and hold the picture. It will be saved with all the other photos on your iPad.

- The Reading List can be used to keep track of articles you'd like to read later.

- The Reader feature is used to strip a web page down to its basics, but it can leave out important content and isn't always available.

# Brain training

How will you fare in the traditional end of chapter quiz?

**1. To put a link to your favourite website on your Home screen, you:**

(a) Add a bookmark to the Bookmarks Bar folder

(b) Create a web clip

(c) Add a bookmark to the website

(d) Tap and hold the address bar

**2. If you want to strip the advertising from a web page so you can read it more easily:**

(a) Add the page to your Reading List

(b) Tap and hold on a link

(c) Tap the Reader button in the address bar

(d) Tap the X on the page's tab

**3. When you finish typing information into one box on a form and want to go to the next, you should:**

(a) Tap the Go key on the keyboard

(b) Tap the Return key on the keyboard

(c) Tap the next form box on the web page

(d) Drag the web page

**4. To view a web page in a new tab, you can:**

(a) Tap the address field

(b) Tap the small tab with a plus sign on it

(c) Tap and hold a link

(d) Double-tap a link

**5. To enlarge the website content, you can:**

(a) Put two fingers on the iPad and move them closer together

(b) Put two fingers on the iPad and move them further apart

(c) Double-tap a column of text

(d) Put your finger on the page and move it up the screen

## Answers

**Q1 –** b          **Q2 –** c          **Q3 –** c          **Q4 –** b and c          **Q5 –** b and c

# PART III
## Sound and vision

I've downloaded our entire music collection from iTunes. Now nobody will be able to see what appalling taste we have.

# Adding music and video to your iPad

**Equipment needed:** An iPad with an Internet connection. Your credit card or an iTunes gift card, if you plan to download from the iTunes store. A computer with a CD drive and an Internet connection, if you want to copy CDs.

**Skills needed:** Experience using apps and gestures. Skills using the web browser (see Chapter 8) are particularly valuable.

One of Apple's shrewdest moves was to create the iTunes store, which sells audio and video content, and makes certain programmes available for free download. The iTunes store was launched in 2003 for iPod music players, and has made Apple one of the most powerful companies in the entertainment business. What it means for you is that you can find Hollywood blockbusters, TV shows, recent or classic albums and educational content, all from the comfort of your sofa.

The content you choose (the programmes, films, and music) is copied straight into your iPad from the Internet, through a process called 'downloading'. Once your music or programmes have been downloaded, they're kept in the iPad so you can play them without needing an Internet connection in future. The process of downloading is fast and convenient. For example, you can discover a new album, hear some samples, buy your favourite songs, download them and start listening to them, all within a few minutes.

There's a fantastic catalogue on offer, including many classic films, TV series and songs that you might have thought you'd never experience again. I've particularly enjoyed watching vintage episodes of Dr Who and downloading rare songs by some of my favourite bands. There's a wealth of music there, from top acts of the 1950s and 1960s to today's chart-toppers. If you've got a favourite record you've lost, or a golden oldie you'd like to hear again, the iTunes store might help.

There is some potential for confusion here: Apple uses the name 'iTunes' to refer both to the software you run on your computer to manage your iPad, and to the store where you buy content for it.

In this chapter, I'll show you how you can use the iTunes store to download audio and video content for your iPad. Even if you don't want to buy music or films, it's worth investigating the iTunes store. As I'll show you, there's lots of free content there too.

What about your CD collection? The good news is that you can use the iTunes software on your computer to copy your music CDs to your iPad. I'll show you how to do that too, so that you'll be ready to explore how to play music and video on your iPad in Chapter 10.

Over 10 billion songs have been downloaded from the iTunes store since it launched. The 10 billionth was *Guess Things Happen That Way* by Johnny Cash, downloaded on 24 February 2010. Coincidentally, that was also the 55th birthday of Steve Jobs, Apple's well-known former chief executive officer.

## Browsing the iTunes store

To get started, tap the iTunes icon on your iPad's Home screen. This is short for 'iTunes store', so when it opens, you'll see something that looks a bit like a shopping website. Figure 9.1 shows you what the store's home page looks like.

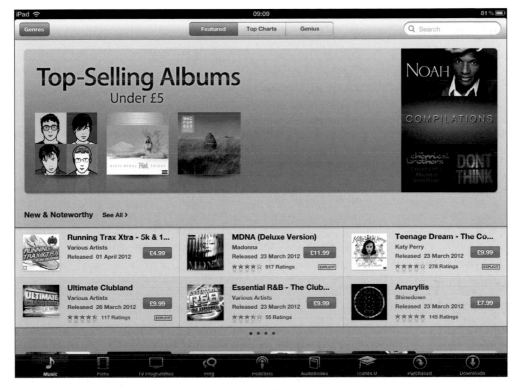

**Figure 9.1**

You navigate the store similar to the way you use a website (see Chapter 8). You can drag the page up to see content that doesn't fit on the screen, and then tap the status bar to jump back to the top of the page. When you see a product or promotion you want to find out more about, tap it to open it the way you do with a link on a web page. At the bottom of the scrolling page, there are buttons to manage your account, redeem gift vouchers or seek support. Across the top of the screen are buttons to select different genres (such as rock, pop or comedy) and to see the bestselling content (tap Top Charts).

Where you see a group of offers, such as those in the bottom half of Figure 9.1, you can often swipe them horizontally to see more. This also applies to the App Store (see Chapter 12) and iBooks store (see Chapter 14).

Along the bottom of the screen, at all times, is a series of buttons that you use to navigate the different types of content in the store. The menu has options for:

● **Music,** which includes music videos and ringtones. Free downloads are made available from time to time, including a free single of the week. But you'll have to pay for nearly all the content in this section. You can find ringtones (just called 'Tones') by tapping Genres in the top left.

● **Films.** You can buy a film, or rent it, which costs less. Buying a film means you can watch it as often as you like, for as long as you like. Rented films expire 48 hours after you start watching them (24 hours in the US), and will then automatically be deleted from your iPad. If you don't get around to watching a film you've rented, it'll be deleted after 30 days anyway.

● **TV Programmes**, including US and UK drama, comedy and children's shows. As with music, there are occasional free downloads, but nearly all the content is for sale.

● **Ping**. This is a place where you can tell other people who use it what you think about certain artists.

● **Podcasts**, which are regular programmes you can download for free. Many radio broadcasters make edited versions of their shows available for free download, for example, but anyone can create a podcast, so there's a lot of material independently published, too. Podcasts can use video or be audio-only. A good place to start is by searching for BBC to find podcasts of Desert Island Discs, Radio 4's Friday Night Comedy, 5 Live Football Daily, The Archers, and many more radio programmes from across the BBC's stations.

● **Audiobooks**, which are professionally recorded readings of books, and radio programmes. You have to pay for these.

● **iTunes U**, which is here for historical reasons. This button just directs you to the free iTunes U app now, which you can use to download free courses from some of the world's leading universities.

● **Purchased**, which enables you to download music and TV shows to your iPad which you've previously bought or downloaded for free from the store (see later in this chapter).

● **Downloads**, which shows you the progress of content you're currently downloading to your iPad.

To search the store, tap the search box in the top right of the screen. It doesn't matter what part of the store you're in when you do this because it will show you results from across the store.

If you're learning a language, you can often download podcasts of language lessons or radio programmes in that language, especially the news.

## Buying music and video from iTunes

We've all bought an album in a shop and felt cheated when we got it home because it only had two good songs on it. On the iTunes store, there's much less risk of this because it allows you to preview the music tracks first, to make sure you like them. You can usually buy individual songs without having to buy the whole album, too. Buying one song is cheaper, but a whole album is often better value than cherry-picking several songs.

Once you've found an album you'd like to buy (by browsing the featured products or using the search), tap its artwork to see the tracks on it. A new window opens in the middle of the screen, as you can see in Figure 9.2. You can drag this window up and down to see more information, including reviews by other customers where available.

To hear a sample of a track, tap its name. You can stop the song playing again by tapping the Stop button that appears in place of its track number. If you don't hear anything, check you have your iPad's volume switched on. To close the album's window and carry on browsing the store, tap outside the album window.

When you've found something you want to buy, tap the price beside the track name; or, to buy the whole album, tap the price underneath the album name at the top (both indicated in Figure 9.2). The Price button will change to a Buy Song or Buy Album button. Tap that, and you'll be prompted to log in to your iTunes account. This is the same account you created when you set up your iPad (see Chapter 2). Usually, your credit card or gift certificate balance will then be charged and your content will be downloaded.

Buy album —

Buy track —

Stop preview —

**Figure 9.2**

The first time you buy something, though, you will also be required to confirm your payment information. You'll be shown your account information, and will need to tap beside where it says 'security code' and enter the three-digit security number on the back of your credit card or the four-digit number on the front of an American Express card. When you've finished confirming your details, tap Done in the top right of the window. You'll get a last chance to back out, but once you tap Buy, your account will be charged and your music will start to download.

> Tap Artist Page, in the top right of an album's window, to quickly find other albums by the same artist. This option isn't shown for compilation albums.

The process for downloading TV shows and films is similar to downloading music. You can search for a particular programme, or browse through the featured titles. When you find something you like, tap its artwork to open its window. The main difference here is that for TV episodes you tap the picture from the episode to see the preview and for films you tap the Preview button on the right.

For video content, you might also be offered two different formats: HD and standard (SD). HD is short for high definition and is a higher quality video format. It looks much sharper on the iPad's screen, but standard definition is acceptable and is the only format available for older TV shows. HD films take longer to download and are usually more expensive than standard definition films.

Films are sometimes released in different definitions at different times. At the time of writing, one of the Harry Potter films can be bought or rented in standard definition, but the HD version is only available to rent.

To download free content, including podcast episodes, tap the Free button that appears in place of a price.

Content is queued up and downloaded one item at a time. It can take several minutes for a film to download, but you can use other apps on your iPad while the downloading continues in the background. To check the progress of your downloads, tap the Downloads button at the bottom of the screen in the iTunes app.

The process of buying is quick and convenient, so much so that you can forget you're spending money. It feels very different to handing over £10 notes in a record shop, so keep an eye on how much you're spending in the iTunes store.

For advice on playing music and video on your iPad, see Chapter 10.

## Using the iTunes store on your computer

If you prefer, you can download content from the iTunes store on your computer. Open the iTunes software on your computer and click iTunes Store on the left. Across the top of the screen are buttons that take you to the different types of content (such as music, films and TV).

There are a few additional features in the iTunes store on your computer. One is that you can add content to a wishlist by clicking the arrow button beside its price. You can view all the items on your wishlist by clicking the arrow beside your email address in the top right.

Another useful addition is that you can subscribe to podcasts, so that your computer automatically downloads the latest episode when you open iTunes. When you view a podcast's details in the iTunes store on your computer, you can click the Free button beside an episode to download just that episode, or click the Subscribe button underneath its artwork to subscribe for free.

When you synchronise your iPad with your computer (see Chapter 2), any content you downloaded on your computer can be copied to your iPad. You can also enable content to automatically download on your iPad over Wi-Fi when you buy it on your computer (see Chapter 2).

## Removing content and downloading it again

Over time, you might find that you've bought more music and video than you can fit on your iPad at the same time, especially if you're a film fan. You can change what's stored on your iPad, though. If you remove some albums or shows to make room on the iPad, you can download them again for free from the store later. Note that you can't download films again (whether you rented them or bought them), but you can keep a copy of bought films on your computer and synchronise them to your iPad from there.

In the case of audio content, you remove it using the Music app. You'll take a more detailed tour of this app next chapter when you learn how to use it to play your music. For now, here's how you delete content using it:

● To delete a song, tap Songs at the bottom of the screen. Find the song you want to remove, and then swipe across it. Tap the Delete button.

● To delete an album, tap Albums at the bottom of the screen. Tap and hold on the album you want to remove and then tap the X button that appears in the top-left corner of its artwork.

● To delete all of an artist's albums, tap Artists at the bottom of the screen. Tap and hold on the artists you want to delete, and then tap the X button in the top-left corner of their artwork.

Films and TV shows take up a lot of space on your iPad, so it's a good idea to delete them from your iPad after watching them. Take care when you delete films, though: if you delete a film that you have rented, it will be permanently deleted and you'll have to pay again to get it back.

To remove films and TV shows from your iPad, you use the Videos app. Again, you'll learn how to use this for playing content next chapter. To delete a programme or series from your iPad, tap and hold its artwork and then tap the X button that appears in its top left. To delete multiple programmes or series, tap the Edit button in the top right when viewing their artwork, and then tap the X button on those you want to remove. When you've finished, tap Done in the top right. To delete an individual episode of a TV series, tap the artwork to view the list of episodes, and then swipe your finger from left to right (or right to left) across the episode summary to reveal the Delete button.

To download music or videos from the store again, go into the iTunes store app and then tap Purchased at the bottom of the screen. This gives you access to iTunes in the Cloud, Apple's service that looks after your music and TV show collection so you can access it on any compatible devices. The screen looks like Figure 9.3. Drag the list of artists on the left and tap one to see the content you've previously downloaded from the store by that artist.

Along the right-hand edge of the artist list, there's an A-Z index (indicated in Figure 9.3) that works like the one in the Contacts app (see Chapter 4). Tap a letter to jump to it, or run your finger down the index to rapidly scroll through the artists.

If you have bought tracks from more than one album, you can tap the Songs or Albums buttons at the top to view the music organised in albums, or as a full song list. You can download a track again by tapping the button with a picture of a cloud on it. There's also a button in the top right to download all the tracks by a particular artist.

By default, you'll see the music you've bought or downloaded, but you can tap the View button in the top left to see videos instead. In that case, programme titles replace the artist names. Tap a programme name, and then tap the series to see individual episodes. You can then download your favourites, or tap the button to download the whole series.

To focus your attention, there's a Not On This iPad button at the top you can tap to see only the content that isn't currently on your iPad. There's also a search box above the artist or programme list so you can quickly find what you're looking for.

Switch between music and video content

A-Z index

Download all tracks by this artist

Download this track

**Figure 9.3**

Apple warns that previous purchases of music, video, apps and books might not be available to download if they've been removed from the store since you bought them. Don't forget you can keep a copy of everything on your computer, and synchronise any content you want from there (see Chapter 2).

# Adding CDs to your iPad using your computer

Of course, most of us have already paid good money to own the music we love, so we'd rather not buy it again. The good news is that you can transfer CDs to your iPad, as long as your computer has a CD drive. Under copyright law, you are only allowed to copy CDs with the permission of whoever created them. However, a lot of people consider it ethical to copy CDs they've bought themselves to their own device for playing them, as long as they continue to own the original CDs. Copying CDs to your computer like this is called 'ripping' them.

Often it's cheaper to buy a CD and rip it using your computer than it is to buy the same album as a download.

To add a CD to your iPad, follow these steps:

1. Start the iTunes software on your computer and insert your music CD in the CD drive.

2. iTunes will download the names of songs and artists from the Internet if possible. If this fails, or you need to correct a piece of information, right-click on a song and choose Get Info from the menu. Click the Info tab and you can then add or edit the song title, band name, genre and year. To change information that applies to all the tracks at the same time, use CTRL+A (PC) or Command+A (Mac) on the keyboard to select them all, then right-click on a track and choose Get Info.

3. Untick any songs you don't wish to copy.

4. Click Import CD in the bottom right. The CD drive will start to whirr, and your CD will be copied to your computer.

If your computer asks you if you want to add the CD to your iTunes library when you insert it, you can just click Yes if the album and song information is correct and you want to copy all the songs.

You can play any CDs you've copied to your computer, and any content you've downloaded from Apple's store, using the iTunes software on your computer as well as your iPad. Find the content you want to play by clicking the content type on the left (for example, music), and then using the search box if necessary in the top right. You can double click a song name to start it playing, and there are CD-player-like controls in the top left to pause and jump forward or back a track.

You can't copy DVDs to your iPad using iTunes, unfortunately, because DVDs have encryption to stop them being copied. There is third-party software available online that you can use to copy DVDs into iTunes.

When you synchronise your iPad with your computer, any CDs you've added to your computer will be copied from your computer to your iPad in accordance with your synchronisation settings (see Chapter 2). If your CD doesn't get copied to your iPad, check that you have set your computer to synchronise either all music or that particular artist, album or genre.

## Using iTunes Match to copy music from your computer to your iPad

iTunes Match is a subscription service provided by Apple which offers the convenience of iTunes in the Cloud for your own music collection. If you have a large CD collection, this service enables you to get access to it easily on your iPad, which means you can play the songs anywhere. It works like this: Apple analyses your music collection, including the CDs you've ripped and any music you've downloaded from rival stores to Apple's, to see whether Apple has the same music in its iTunes catalogue. If it does, it'll make a note that you've bought this music and let you download it on your iPad. If not, Apple will copy your music to a storage area on the Internet. The end result is that Apple will let you download any of your music on your iPad at any time, whether or not you originally bought that music from Apple.

To download the music, you need to have an Internet connection, but music you download will stay on your iPad as long as there is space, so you can play it later without having an Internet connection.

This service is only available if you have fewer than 25,000 songs that weren't bought from iTunes, so it's not for the most ardent music fans with large CD collections!

To use iTunes Match, go to the iTunes software on your computer and click iTunes Match on the left. Click the Subscribe button (the current price is £21.99 per year) and log in with your Apple ID to make the purchase. The process of analysing your collection and uploading unknown tracks might take a while: for a collection of about 3,000 songs, the whole process took about six hours. You can continue to use your computer and iTunes while this is going on, though.

You need to turn on iTunes Match on your iPad, so go into the Settings app, tap Music on the left and then turn iTunes Match on. You can't use iTunes Match together with music synchronised from your computer (nor do you need to), so any existing music will be removed.

When you go into the Music app, you'll see your entire collection available to play. When you play a song, it is downloaded to your iPad. You can also download songs without playing them using the buttons with clouds on them, like those in Figure 9.3. If there isn't a download button next to a particular song, that means it's already stored on your iPad.

When you run out of room on your iPad, iTunes Match will automatically remove some songs you haven't played for a while to make room. However, they remain stored in iTunes Match so you can always download them again later.

Now that you've learned how to add music and video to your iPad, in the next chapter we'll look at how you can play it.

One popular way of storing music on a computer is in a file called an MP3, and your iPad can play any song in that format. You can buy MP3 music downloads from Amazon using your computer. When you search in Amazon for a particular album or artist, you will often be given the choice to download an MP3 album instead of buying a CD. Amazon provides some free software that will copy the MP3s you buy to your iTunes software for you automatically. You can't buy music downloads from Amazon on your iPad. Instead, shop on your computer, and your purchases can be copied to your iPad by synchronising with your computer or using iTunes Match. Amazon often has a different product range and pricing structure to the iTunes store, so it's worth shopping around.

## Summary

- You can download music and video content from the iTunes store, either on your iPad or by using your computer.

- You have to pay for most content, but you can download podcasts and the single of the week for free.

- You navigate the store similar to the way you navigate a website.

- You can buy individual songs or TV episodes, or a whole album or TV series.

- For a brief sample before you buy on your iPad, tap the name of the music track, the picture of the TV show or the Film Preview button.

- High definition films and TV programmes are better quality, but older films and programmes are only available in standard definition.

- High definition content is much larger than standard definition content, and will take longer to download.

- You can delete music and TV shows you've bought from iTunes from your iPad, and download it again later.

- You can copy your music CDs to your computer using the iTunes software on it. Then you can copy the music to your iPad from your computer when you synchronise your iPad with your computer.

- The iTunes Match service analyses your music collection on your computer and enables you to download any music you own on your iPad any time you have an Internet connection.

# Brain training

Hopefully, your iPad is now packed full of great videos and music you can enjoy. Use this quick quiz to check whether you've mastered the art of adding music and video to your iPad.

**1. You can buy content for your iPad using:**

(a) The Music app on your iPad

(b) The iTunes app on your iPad

(c) The iTunes software on your computer

(d) The App Store app on your iPad

**2. To be able to watch a Hollywood film on your iPad whenever you like and as often as you like, you can:**

(a) Rip a DVD using iTunes

(b) Buy a film in the iTunes store

(c) Rent a film in the iTunes store

(d) Download in high definition

**3. To play the CDs you've ripped to your computer on your iPad, you can:**

(a) Synchronise your iPad with your computer

(b) Go into the iTunes store app and tap Purchased

(c) Subscribe to iTunes Match

(d) Tap and hold on an album's artwork

**4. If you tap the price beside a song in the iTunes app, it will:**

(a) Start a preview of that song

(b) Start the buying process for that album

(c) Start the buying process for that song

(d) Download that album to your computer

**5. If you tap the picture beside a TV episode in the iTunes app, it will:**

(a) Enlarge the picture

(b) Show you the chapters in that episode

(c) Start the buying process for that episode

(d) Play a preview of the episode

## Answers

**Q1** – b and c     **Q2** – b     **Q3** – a and c     **Q4** – c     **Q5** – d

# Playing audio and video on your iPad

**10**

**Equipment needed:** An iPad with audio and/or video content loaded onto it (see Chapter 9), and/or an Internet connection for watching YouTube videos. Earphones if you'd like to use them.

**Skills needed:** Good command of gestures, including tapping and dragging.

The iPad enables you to take your favourite music and videos with you wherever you go, and gives you a number of interesting new ways to enjoy your music collection. If there is one track in the middle of your favourite album that really niggles you, or if you've always wanted a jukebox that plays your favourite songs in a random order, the playlists feature can help.

The iPad's high-quality screen is also ideal for watching films, whether these are full-length movies you've bought or rented, or short films published on the Internet.

In this chapter, I'll show you how to play music and video on your iPad. I'll assume you've successfully added music or video to your iPad, by downloading it from the iTunes store or by ripping music from your CDs. Both of these were covered in Chapter 9, so refer back there for a refresher if necessary. If you haven't added any videos to your iPad, you can still try watching videos with the YouTube app, as I'll show you. You'll also learn how to play podcasts and audiobooks.

# Playing audio content on your iPad

The app used to play music is called simply 'Music' and you can find it on the dock at the bottom of your Home screen. Tap it to start.

You can choose whether you want to listen to your music using earphones (which you'll need to buy separately) or not. If you have earphones, plug them into the round hole on the back of your iPad. It's in the top-left corner when the Home button is at the bottom.

## Browsing and playing your music

The Music app gives you several different ways to browse through your music collection. By default, you see your content sorted by Songs, but you can tap the buttons at the bottom of the screen (See Figure 10.1) to see your music organised by Artists or Albums. The numbers beside tracks (such as 5:11 and 2:12 in Figure 10.1) are the length of the track in minutes and seconds.

If you tap the More button, a menu opens so you can choose to view your music by genres or composers, see your podcasts or audiobooks, or choose whether the music is sorted by its title or by the artist name. The Composers view is particularly useful if you're a classical music fan, but most rock and pop music fans will rarely stray from the Songs, Artists and Albums views. To see your list of songs again, tap the Songs button at the bottom of the screen.

You can drag the song list up and down, or use the search in the bottom right to find a particular track, album or artist. When you've found something you want to play, just tap the song name and it will start to play. A speaker appears next to that track in the song list, and its artist, track name and album name are shown at the top of the screen in the centre. Your music will continue to play even if you put the iPad into sleep mode, or if you press the Home button and go into another app. If you want to stop it playing again, go back into the Music app and tap the Pause/Play button (see Figure 10.1).

At the top of the screen are various playback controls, indicated in Figure 10.1. In the top right, there is a volume indicator and control. Drag the circle left to turn the volume down, or right to turn it up. You can also use the physical volume switch on your iPad (see Chapter 2) to change the volume and move the indicator. You can also press the Home button twice quickly and then swipe from left to right at the bottom of the screen to reveal the volume controls when you're not using the Music app.

Figure 10.1

If you can't hear anything, always check the volume first. It's almost too obvious to say, but we've all spent time shaking and tuning radios that just needed their volume nudged up.

In the top left are playback controls that are similar to those you might have seen marked on a CD player. The central button is used to start or pause playing. Tap the button to the left of it (indicated as the Back button in Figure 10.1) once to restart playing the current track from the beginning, or twice to go to the previous track. The button to the right of the Pause/Play button (the Forward button in Figure 10.1) skips to the next track.

You can also tap and hold these two buttons to fast forward or rewind through a track, but it's easier to use the playhead control to the right, which shows the progress of the playback. You can drag this left or right to go to any position in the song. The bar it slides in is always the same length whether the song lasts for 3 minutes or 30 minutes, so nudging the playhead a centimetre along the bar could advance the song a few seconds or a minute or more depending on the song's length. Sliding it to midway along the bar will always be halfway through the song, though.

Have a go at playing a few tracks, just to familiarise yourself with how the Music app works.

Tap the Artists button at the bottom to see your music alphabetically sorted by artist, with details of how many songs and albums you have by each artist. Because the iPad can't tell the difference between the name of a person and the name of a band, it doesn't sort artists by surname, as you might expect. Instead, it sorts everything from the first letter of the first word, which means Paul McCartney comes after Frank Zappa. This can throw you a bit at first, but it makes a lot more sense than hunting for Pink Floyd under F or having the Rolling Stones under S. An exception to this sorting method is that iTunes ignores the word 'The', so you will still find The Beatles under B. If you tap the name of an artist, you can see which of their tracks and albums you have on your iPad. Tap any one of these to play it.

The Albums view is the most attractive (see Figure 10.2), showing the artwork for all your albums arranged in rows. As with the Songs and Artists view, you can drag up and down to see more. When you tap an album, a large central panel opens to show you the tracks on it, and you can tap a track name to start that song playing.

**Figure 10.2**

The different views aren't purely cosmetic: when one song finishes, they also decide what song will play next. If you choose the Songs view, the next song will be the next song alphabetically according to the song title, no matter who the artist is, even if you've sorted the songs by artist. In the Albums and Artists views, it's the next song on the same album. If you have used the search box in the bottom right, the next song to play will be the next one in the list of search results.

## Looping and shuffling your music

When a song is playing, there are two different ways the iPad will behave. It will either have the song's artwork filling its screen or show a small version of the artwork beside the Forward button, so you can continue browsing your music on screen. If you tap the small artwork (indicated in Figure 10.1), you can make it fill the screen, as in Figure 10.3.

Album artwork © Tom Hingley

**Figure 10.3**

When the artwork is filling the screen (the 'artwork view'), you can tap it to reveal the standard playback controls. There are some new controls at the bottom too (indicated in Figure 10.3):

● **Show songs on this album**: Tap the button in the bottom right to see all the songs on the same album as the song that's playing. In this view, you can also rate your music, giving it one to five stars by tapping one of the five dots underneath the playhead control.

● **Close artwork view**: Tap this to go back to the Songs, Artists, Albums, Genres or Composers view.

> You can swipe the artwork left and right to move between the previous and next songs.

There are a couple of extra controls you can use too, indicated in Figure 10.3. You can use them any time you're listening to your music on the iPad:

- **Looping**: Tap this once to replay the list of songs from the beginning when it reaches the end of the list. When you tap it, the icon will go orange. You can also ask it to repeat the current song by tapping it again; a 1 will appear on the icon, and the song currently playing will repeat until you stop it. Tap the icon again to turn off looping.

- **Shuffle**: This plays the songs in a random order. Tap it once to activate it (the icon goes orange) and tap it again to turn it off.

## Creating a playlist on your iPad

One of the best features of digital music is that it allows you to create your own playlists, which enable you to cue up a list of songs you'd like to hear. You could create a playlist of background music for a party, a set of songs that put you in a good mood, or a list of your favourite tracks from a particular artist. The lists can be as short or long as you like, and you can put the songs in any order you like. You can use the shuffle feature to listen to a playlist, too, to mix up the order songs are played in and add an element of surprise.

To create a playlist on your iPad, follow these steps:

1. Tap the Playlists button at the bottom of the screen and then tap New in the top right.

2. Think of a name for your playlist, type it in, and tap Save. You'll often only see the first few words of a playlist's name onscreen, so make sure these are distinctive.

3. You'll see the list of all the songs on your iPad, but now you'll see there is a plus icon beside each song. To add a song to your playlist, tap its entry in the song list. If you tap more than once, the song will be added to the list as many times as you tap it. Songs that you've added to the playlist are shown in a light grey colour. You don't have to add songs in the Songs view – you can also choose songs by Artist, Album, Genre or Composer, by tapping the buttons at the bottom of the screen. You can use the search box to find particular songs or artists too.

4. Once you've chosen all the songs you want to be in this particular playlist, tap Done in the top right. You'll see your playlist (see Figure 10.4), with a red Delete button beside each song. Tap this to remove any songs you don't want in your playlist any more. (Don't worry – this won't delete them from your iPad, only from this playlist.)

5. It's easy to change a song's place in the list: just tap and hold its three-bar icon on the right and move your finger up or down the screen. When you release your finger, the song will be dropped into that position in the playlist.

6. To add more songs, tap Add Songs in the top right. When you've finished, tap Done in the top right.

**Figure 10.4**

To go to your playlist, tap the Playlists button at the bottom of the screen and then tap its name. You can then start playing from any track, or tap the Shuffle button at the top of the playlist to hear the songs in a random order. If you want to add more songs or take some out, go to your playlist and then tap Edit in the top right.

The iPad also has a feature called Genius, which is another way you can create playlists. If you first choose a song you like and then tap the Genius Playlist button, it will automatically generate a playlist of other songs that should sound good with your chosen song. To use Genius, you first need to enable it in iTunes on your computer (click Store on the menu and then click Turn on Genius). Once it's enabled, this will periodically send information about your music collection to Apple, which Apple analyses to create automatic playlists for you but may also use to recommend products to you. After turning on Genius on your computer, you need to synchronise your iPad with your computer (see Chapter 2) so you can use Genius on your iPad. The Genius feature is only useful if you have a music collection on your computer.

You can also create more sophisticated playlists using the iTunes software on your computer. These playlists can automatically compile your most popular, least popular, most often played, or least often played songs and combine that with information about the music itself, to create your top 60s pop hits, for example. For a guide to creating playlists using iTunes, see **www. pcwisdom.co.uk**.

## Playing podcasts and audiobooks

As well as music, you play your audio podcasts and audiobooks in the Music app. Tap More at the bottom and the menu lets you browse Podcasts or Audiobooks (see Figure 10.1). You play an episode or a book in the same way as you play a song, by tapping its name.

If you use Apple's iTunes U app to download university lectures for free, you can also find and play them through the More menu, but it's probably easier to play this content from the iTunes U app.

There are two additional controls available when you're playing podcasts, audio-books and iTunes U lectures, shown in Figure 10.5. You can tap the Playback Speed button to change between normal speed (1x), double speed (2x) or half speed (0.5x), so you can whizz through the boring bits; and there's a button to rewind 30 seconds in case you miss something important.

Rewind 30 seconds

Playback speed

**Figure 10.5**

# Watching videos on your iPad

In Chapter 9, you learned how to add video content to your iPad, such as vintage TV shows and Hollywood blockbusters. If you have an iPad with cameras, you'll also be able to shoot videos on it, as you'll see in Chapter 11.

There are three different apps that are used to play video on your iPad:

● **Videos**: This app is used to watch videos you've bought or downloaded from iTunes (see Chapter 9). If you try to play a music video in the Music app, you'll hear the music but won't see the video.

● **YouTube**: This app enables you to watch short films from the video-sharing website **www.youtube.com**. Anyone can publish a video on YouTube, so the site features lots of homemade movies as well as content from major broadcasters. Whether or not you have downloaded any videos using the iTunes store, you can always watch free online films from YouTube.

● **Photos**: This app is used to watch videos you've filmed using your iPad, if you have an iPad with cameras, as you'll learn in Chapter 11.

In this section, I'll tell you more about how you can watch video on your iPad.

## Using the Videos app

You will find the Videos app on your Home screen. When you start it, you can choose what type of content you want to watch (a movie, TV show, video podcast, music video or iTunes U course) by tapping the appropriate button at the top. As with audio content, it's easier to use the iTunes U courses from within their dedicated app, but you can find them here too for convenience.

Each show is represented by its artwork or a still image taken from it (see Figure 10.6). If there are too many programmes to fit in one screenful, you can drag the page up to see more.

**Figure 10.6**

To start viewing a programme, tap its artwork or still image. If you choose a TV show, you'll then be shown all the episodes of that show on your iPad, and you can tap a particular show to start playing it. If you tap the round Play button at the top, it will begin playing the whole series from the start.

When you tap a movie's artwork, you see information about the film, which might include its summary and cast list. There's a round Play button to start the film from the beginning. If you like, you can often skip ahead to a particular 'chapter' (section) of the film. Tap the Chapters button, drag the chapters list to find the one you want and then tap it to start the film from that point.

If you tap Get More Episodes, you'll be taken into iTunes to download or buy more content from the same series or podcast.

While a video is playing, you can tap the screen to show the controls. These are similar to the YouTube controls shown in Figure 10.7, which we will come to later. At the bottom, there are Back and Forward buttons, which you tap and hold to rewind or fast forward. If the video has chapters, you can tap these buttons to skip through them, as well: tap the Back button once to start from the beginning of the current chapter, and tap it again to jump to the previous chapter. Tap the Forward button to advance to the next chapter.

Between the two Back and Forward buttons is a Play/Pause button and underneath them is a slider to control the volume. You can also use the physical volume control on the side of your iPad.

At the top is a playhead slider you can use to see how far through the programme you are, and to move through the programme.

If you're watching a widescreen programme, you can double-tap the screen to change between widescreen mode (which leaves black spaces at the top and bottom of the screen) and standard mode (which chops off the sides of the image so it can fill the screen).

In the top left is a Done button, which will take you back to the Videos app so you can choose what video you'd like to play next. Your iPad remembers how much of a TV show, film, podcast or iTunes U course you've watched, so when you come back to a programme next time, it will start playing from where you left off. To play a film from the start, tap the first chapter. For a TV programme or other video without chapters, start it playing and then tap the Back button to go back to the start.

## Watching online films from YouTube

The Videos app will work wherever you are, but you'll need an Internet connection to use the YouTube app. That's because YouTube films are downloaded from the Internet and you don't save them but watch them as they're downloading. Because the programmes aren't stored on your iPad permanently, you can happily watch YouTube until your eyes go square – unlike content you buy from the iTunes store, for which there's a limit to how much will fit in your iPad.

YouTube is free to watch, and there's a wealth of comedy, tutorial and dramatic content on there. There are full length films and programmes, but most YouTube videos are just a few minutes long, making them perfect for snacking on between other programmes.

Anyone can put videos on YouTube, including members of the public. YouTube says that more video is uploaded to YouTube in one month than the three major US TV networks created in 60 years. A total of 60 hours of video are uploaded to YouTube every minute and over 4 billion videos are viewed every day.

Start the YouTube app and you'll see a selection of featured videos, which you can drag up to see more. You can tap the buttons at the bottom of the screen to explore the top rated and most viewed films. There's also a button you can use to quickly find any films you've marked as your favourites.

Most of the time, though, you'll want to use the search box in the top right to find something to watch. Try entering some words relating to your hobbies or interests;

or, if you know the user name of a friend who posts content on YouTube, try entering that. The screen will fill with film suggestions. For each one, there is a still picture, the length (for example, '03:44' means three minutes and 44 seconds) and how many times the video has been viewed. Tap a film and it will start to play.

As with the Videos app, the controls fade away so you can concentrate on the film, but you can bring them back by tapping the screen. Because the film has to download from the Internet, it can take a moment or two before it begins to play. The runner for the playhead control along the top of the screen fills with grey to show how much of the video has downloaded to the iPad.

**Figure 10.7**

Figure 10.7 shows the YouTube player in action. This short film is a trailer created to promote the first edition of this book. Most of the controls indicated in Figure 10.7 will be familiar to you from the Videos and Music apps. There are a few additional controls, however: you can add videos to your favourites so you can quickly find them later, and you can tap the Show Information button to see more information about the film while it plays.

When the film finishes playing, the app takes you to the information page for the film you've been viewing (see Figure 10.8). Underneath the film, you can read a summary of it, provided by the person who published the film on YouTube. Across the top of the film are buttons you can use to add it to your favourites, share the video (by email or using Twitter), or give a video the thumbs up, or thumbs down.

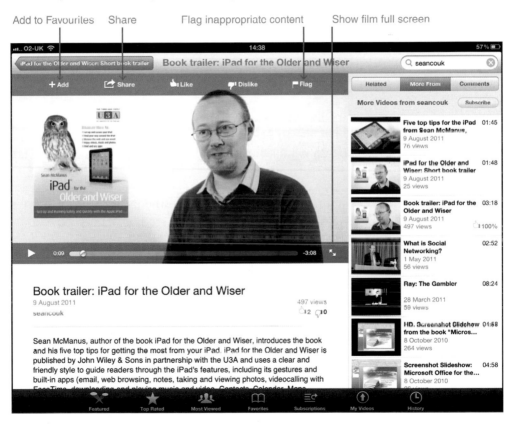

**Figure 10.8**

Although anyone can share films on YouTube, I've never come across anything inappropriate. If you did find objectionable or illegal content on YouTube, you could report it by tapping Flag, to flag inappropriate content to the service's owners. To block younger family members from using YouTube, use restrictions in the Settings app to disable YouTube (see Chapter 2).

You can watch films on YouTube as much as you want without having an account, but certain features are restricted to registered users. You'll need to register before you're able to tap the Like or Dislike buttons, add comments to videos or publish your own films. To get your free account, visit www. youtube.com using the Safari app (see Chapter 8) or your main computer. YouTube is owned by Google, so if you have already registered for other Google services (such as a Gmail email address) you can use that account for YouTube also.

The column on the right of the information page helps you find other films to watch. If you want to see what else the same film-maker has made, tap More From at the top. If you prefer to see what others have filmed on a similar theme, tap Related.

Also on the right, the Comments button shows you comments from other viewers and gives you a chance to add your own. Any comments you enter can be read by anyone on the Internet, so take care about what information you share here.

There are free apps available for watching TV shows you missed, including BBC iPlayer, Channel 4's 4oD and ITV Player. Netflix and Lovefilm both offer apps for watching films on your iPad too if you pay a subscription fee. See Chapter 12 for advice on finding and downloading apps.

## Summary

- The Music app is used to play audio content on your iPad.

- You can browse and play your music by Songs, Artists, Albums, Genres or Composers.

- Shuffle plays an album, playlist or other music selection in a random order.

- You can loop a list of songs or an individual song so it plays over and over again.

- You can create playlists on your iPad or on your computer.

- The Videos app is used to play videos downloaded from the iTunes store.

- When a video is playing, tap the screen to show the playback controls.

- The YouTube app shows you free short films on the Internet.

- Some features in the YouTube app are only available after you register at the YouTube website.

# Brain training

The iPad is a fantastic entertainment device, and a great way to enjoy music, films and educational content. Refresh your knowledge of the key points in this chapter with a quick quiz.

**1. The playhead control is used to:**

(a) Move to a different point in a song

(b) Skip to the next track

(c) Show how much of a YouTube video has downloaded

(d) Create a playlist

**2. To watch videos downloaded from the iTunes store, you use:**

(a) The YouTube app

(b) The Videos app

(c) The iTunes app

(d) Any of the above

**3. You tap and hold the Forward button to:**

(a) Skip to the next song

(b) Skip to the next film chapter

(c) Fast forward through a song to the guitar solo

(d) Fast forward through a boring bit in a film

**4. If you tap the 1x button when listening to an audiobook:**

(a) It will repeat that section once

(b) It will change the speed of playback

(c) It will replay the last 30 seconds

(d) It will reset the volume

**5. You need to register a YouTube account to:**

(a) Publish your own videos on YouTube

(b) Add comments to videos

(c) Watch videos on YouTube

(d) Search videos on YouTube

## Answers

**Q1** – a and c      **Q2** – b      **Q3** – c and d      **Q4** – b      **Q5** – a and b

# PART IV
## Getting creative with the iPad

Don't the photos of you and Mark
look fantastic on this iPad! You can
see every little wrinkle!

# Taking and browsing photos on your iPad

**11**

**Equipment needed:** Any iPad, to view photos and copy them from your computer or from a digital camera. An iPad with built-in cameras, if you want to take photos with your iPad.

**Skills needed:** Familiarity with starting and using apps, with using on-screen controls and with gestures including pinch and flick.

The iPad's large, high-quality screen is perfect for showing off your digital photographs to friends and family, and for making simple edits to them. In this chapter, you'll learn how to browse and edit your photos on your iPad.

The second and third generation iPads have two cameras: one on the front of the device and one on the back. The camera was greatly improved on the third generation iPad, but it's still not as good as the camera on an iPhone or a modern digital camera. Nevertheless, the cameras are handy for capturing informal shots, especially if you carry your iPad everywhere but don't usually travel with a camera. If you have an iPad with cameras, I'll show you how to take still photos and videos with it.

If not, you can still enjoy viewing and editing photos on the iPad. See Chapter 2 for advice on copying photos from your computer to your iPad.

If you want to take a picture (a screenshot) of what's on your iPad's screen, press and release the Home button and the Wake/Sleep button at the same time. It takes practice to do this without turning the iPad off!

# Using the cameras on your iPad

If you have a first generation iPad without cameras, skip ahead to 'Viewing photos on your iPad'.

It's easy to take photos with the iPad. To begin, start the Camera app. You'll be asked whether the app can use your current location. If you agree, photos and videos will be tagged (labelled) with the location where they were taken. That allows you to browse them on a map later, which is a nice alternative to a photo album or slide show.

## Taking photos on your iPad

When you use the Camera app, the screen is almost filled with a view through one of the cameras. Figure 11.1 shows the camera app in action. Apple has moved some of the buttons around in a software update, so see Chapter 2 for guidance on updating your iPad's software if necessary.

If you can't recognise what's on screen, check that you don't have your finger or something else obstructing the lens, and move the iPad around to make sure that it's not pointing at a wall or ceiling. It's easier to use the back camera if you detach the smart cover.

**Figure 11.1**

Here's how to take a photo using your iPad:

1. Tap the Swap Cameras button in the bottom right to change between the front and back cameras. The back camera (on the opposite side to the screen) is higher quality than the front.

2. If you want to show grid lines to help you to compose your shot (see Figure 11.1), tap Options at the bottom of the screen, and then tap the On button to enable the grid. The Options button changes to a Done button, so tap that to hide the options again. The grid is just an onscreen aid and won't show up on your pictures.

3. Frame your shot. Line up the iPad so it's pointing at what you want to photograph. Remember that if you want a photo of someone looking at the camera (including yourself, if you use the front camera), they need to look into the lens when the photo is taken, and not at the screen or back of the iPad.

4. Set the focal point. Tap the most important part of the picture, and a box will show on it (see Figure 11.1). The iPad uses this to set the focus and exposure for the picture. If you tap and hold until the box pulses, you can lock the exposure and focus and then move the iPad to recompose your shot. If you opened the options to find the grid control, you'll need to close them again to be able to focus. The third generation iPad automatically detects up to ten faces in the picture and balances the focus and exposure across them. Each identified face is shown with a green box.

5. Set the zoom. To zoom in and out, you simply use the same pinch gesture you use to enlarge web pages (see Chapter 8). When you pinch, a zoom control appears at the bottom of the screen too, which you can slide from left to right to zoom in and out. Zoom is only available for the back camera.

6. You can just tap the Take Picture button to take the shot, but that often knocks the camera and spoils the composition, so it's better to put your finger on the button and steady the camera. When you lift your finger from the button, the picture will be taken. Alternatively, you can use the Volume Up button on the edge of the iPad to take a picture. It makes the iPad feel more like a camera, but the button is quite close to the lens, so you need to take care to make sure your fingers don't obscure the lens. When you take a picture, you'll see the aperture close on screen briefly, and will hear a shutter sound unless you have muted your iPad (see Chapter 2).

To view your photos, tap the Review Shots button in the bottom left, which shows a tiny version of the last picture you shot. When you tap it, it takes you to your Camera Roll album, which stores images created on the iPad, including any pictures you've saved from websites. The way you navigate this album is the same as the Photos app, which I'll show you later this chapter. There's an additional button, though: when you've finished reviewing your photos, you can tap Done in the top right to go back into the Camera app.

You can also swipe across the screen to go from from the camera to the last photo taken, and keep swiping to browse the photos taken before that. Swipe from left to right to go back through your photos, and from right to left to view more recent photos and finally return to the camera.

## Shooting videos with your iPad

The Camera app can also be used to shoot high definition (HD) video. In the bottom right of the screen is a switch to choose between taking still images and shooting video (see Figure 11.1). When you slide the switch from the camera icon to the video camera icon, the Take Picture button changes to a Record button. Tap it to start filming, and tap it again when you want to stop. While you are recording, the button will flash. You can't use the zoom when you are shooting video.

This is a bit confusing: you won't be able to see any of the videos you've made while you're in the Videos app. Instead, they are kept in your photo album, so you browse and play them using the Photos app.

## Using Photo Booth for special effects

The Photo Booth app, which comes with the iPad, enables you to take photos with special effects applied to them, such as x-ray, mirror effects, kaleidoscope or a simulated thermal camera. When you start the app, you can see the effects that are available on the camera. Tap one of the effects, and you go into the camera with that effect applied – for example, Figure 11.2 shows a picture of a piano taken with the simulated thermal effect.

You can use either camera to do this, by tapping the Swap Cameras button in the bottom right (see Figure 11.2). There's no focus or exposure setting in Photo Booth. If you're going to mash people's faces around or colour trees blue, there doesn't seem much point! You can adjust the non-colour effects (mirror, kaleidoscope, twirl, squeeze, light tunnel, and stretch) by pinching and/or dragging the screen. To take a picture, just point your iPad, and tap the Take Picture button at the bottom centre of the screen. To try a different effect, tap the button in the bottom left.

Your photos automatically go into your Camera Roll album. At the bottom of the screen, you can see small versions of the pictures you've taken, called thumbnails. You can drag the thumbnail strip left and right to view all the pictures you've taken in Photo Booth. If you tap one, it will fill the screen. You can then tap the Delete button (a cross in a circle) on its thumbnail to get rid of it, or tap the Take Picture button to get back to taking photos.

When you view a photo, the controls disappear after a moment so you can see the entire image. To bring the controls back, tap the picture.

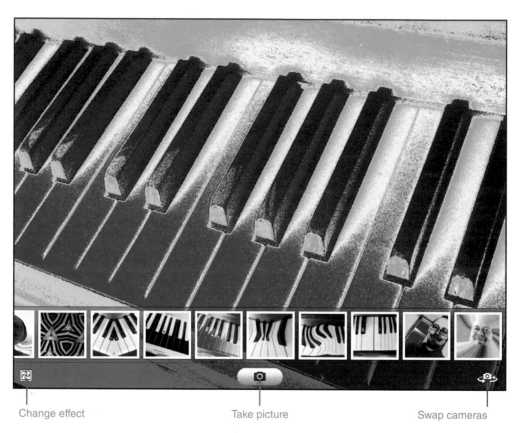

Change effect            Take picture            Swap cameras

**Figure 11.2**

If you want to email your creations to someone, tap one of the thumbnails, and then tap the Use Photo button that appears in the bottom right corner, in place of the Swap Cameras button. You can then tap any of the thumbnails to select them (tap again to de-select), and tap Email to send them in a new email message. Who can you surprise with a weirdly warped family portrait?

# Viewing photos on your iPad

Whether you take photos using your iPad, or copy them from your camera or computer, the iPad is ideal for showing them off. The Photos app is designed to do exactly that, so fire it up to get started.

You can use the iPad Camera Connection Kit (sold separately) to copy photos from your digital camera to your iPad. Visit **www.pcwisdom.co.uk** for a guide to using it.

As you can see in Figure 11.3, your photos are organised in several different ways. You can tap the Places button at the top to see your photos arranged on a map. This uses positioning data stored in the photo when you take a photo using an iPad if you enable location services. More impressively, it will also pick up place names in any descriptive tags you've added to your photos using Windows or a program like iPhoto or Adobe Photoshop Elements. Tap a pin on the map to see one of the photos taken there, and then tap that picture to see them all.

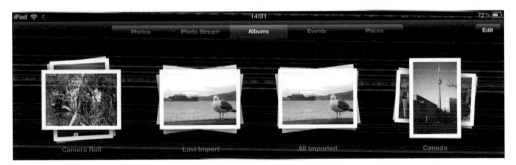

**Figure 11.3**

The Photo Stream feature of iCloud enables you to share your photos with other devices. If you enable Photo Stream on your iPad, the photos you take will be sent to your other devices (such as your computer) automatically, and will appear there as soon as a minute or two after you take them. You can also allow photos to be copied to your iPad automatically from your iPhone, iPod touch or computer. Tap Photo Stream at the top of the iPad screen to see all the photos in Photo Stream, both those taken on the iPad and those sent from other devices. See Chapter 2 for tips on setting up iCloud and Photo Stream.

Using the Events option at the top of the screen (see Figure 11.3), you can see photos you have imported from your camera organised by date. This option doesn't appear for photos you've synchronised from your computer or photos you've taken using your iPad.

You can also tap Photos to see all of the pictures on your iPad, or Albums to see your photos organised in folders. The folders you see on your iPad will depend on what pictures you have on there and how they got there, but they might include:

● **Camera Roll:** This stores images created on your iPad, including photos you've taken using it.

● **All Imported:** This includes all the photos you have imported from your digital camera or SD card, if you have the iPad Camera Connection Kit.

● **Last Import:** This album makes it easy to find the last batch of photos you imported from your camera using the iPad Camera Connection Kit.

● **Folders from your computer:** If you synchronise with your computer using the iTunes software on it, any photos you copy will be organised in the same folders they were on your PC. In Figure 11.3, the 'Canada' folder has been synchronised from my PC using the iTunes software on it. Your iPad might also show the albums used to organise your photos on your computer in software such as iPhoto on the Mac and Photoshop Elements in Windows.

The Photos button at the top of the screen provides easy access to all your photos, including all those from your computer, irrespective of which folder they're in.

Tap an album, and thumbnails of all the photos in it will appear. Tap a photo, or use the pinch gesture to enlarge it, and it will expand to fill the screen. You can use the pinch gesture to zoom (see Chapter 8), and can drag the enlarged picture around to see different parts of it. When you rotate your iPad, the picture rotates too. If you use the iPad in the same orientation as the photo (for example, viewing a landscape-shaped picture with the iPad in landscape orientation), the picture will enlarge to fill the screen.

Figure 11.4 shows the controls available to you when you're looking at a photo. They are:

- **Album browser**: See another photo in this album by touching its tiny thumbnail at the bottom of the screen. You can just roll your finger along this strip of thumbnails. You can also flick the main photo that fills the screen to the left to see the next photo, or flick right to see the previous one in the album.

- **Delete photo**: This control is used to delete a photo from your iPad. If you delete a photo from the Photo Stream folder, it will also be deleted from other devices that use your Photo Stream, such as your computer. You cannot delete photos that have been synchronised from your computer using the iTunes software: to remove them from your iPad, you have to remove them from the folder or album on your computer that is synchronised with your iPad. Then, when you next synchronise your iPad with your computer, the photos will be removed from your iPad.

- **Use photo**: Tap this to email the photo, send it in a message (see Chapter 7), set it as your iPad wallpaper, assign it to one of your contacts (see Chapter 4), print it, or copy it so you can paste it into another app. If you use the Twitter social network, you can also tweet it from here.

- **Back**: The button in the top left will take you back to the album so you can see thumbnails for all the pictures in it. In Figure 11.4, it says 'Camera Roll' because that's the name of the album this photo is in. You can also use a pinch (zoom out) gesture to close a photo and go back to the album. When you're looking at the album, a button in the top left takes you back to see all your albums so you can choose another one.

If you admire your photo for a moment or two, the controls will disappear so you can see it clearly. To bring them back, tap the photo. You can double-tap a point on the photo to zoom in on it and double-tap the screen again to zoom out.

Back

Edit photo  Slideshow  Use photo

Delete
photo

Album
browser

**Figure 11.4**

# Watching a slideshow

A slideshow is a great way to enjoy your photos. You can start it running and then hand the iPad to a friend to watch, or use the iPad Smart Cover to stand up your iPad so it works like a digital photo frame.

To start a slideshow featuring photos from the album you're browsing, tap the Slideshow button in the top right, indicated in Figure 11.4, and a menu opens.

A number of special effects (called transitions) are used between the photos, and you can tap to choose from several different effects. They range from the simple Dissolve, where one photo fades into another, to the elaborate Origami, where your photos are combined into collages that fold like pieces of paper.

If you have music on your iPad, you can choose a song to accompany your slide-show, by switching the Play Music switch on and then tapping Music underneath to pick a song.

Tap Start Slideshow and the slideshow will begin. You can tap the screen to stop it again.

You can change how long each slide is shown for, and whether photos repeat or appear in a random order (shuffle). Go into the Settings app, and tap Photos on the left.

The iPad also has a photo frame option, which you can use without unlocking your iPad. This works independently of slideshows in the Photos app, so to change the transition, timings and photos shown, go into the Settings app and tap Picture Frame on the left. To start the Picture Frame when your iPad is locked, instead of sliding to unlock it, tap the Picture Frame button in the bottom right (this looks like a picture of a flower).

The Picture Frame feature is set to show all photos by default, which could be a privacy threat. Because you can use Picture Frame when the iPad is locked, anyone can use the Picture Frame feature, even if your iPad is pro tected with a passcode. In the Settings app, you can choose to restrict the Picture Frame so that it only shows folders of photos that you don't mind anyone seeing. You can also turn the Picture Frame off by going into the General Settings, and tapping Passcode Lock.

## Organising your photos in albums

To make it easier to organise your photos for viewing, you can create albums and add photos to them. Because you can show slideshows of an album, and the

Picture Frame can be set to show only a particular album (in the Settings app), creating an album is a good way to sort photos before displaying them. Any folders you create on your iPad aren't synchronised back to your computer, though. Here's how to create an album:

1. Go into the Photos app.

2. If the app shows a photo full-screen, tap in the top left to go to that photo's album and then tap in the top left again to see all albums.

3. Tap Albums at the top of the screen and then tap Edit in the top right.

4. Tap New Album in the top left.

5. Enter a name for your new album in the box that appears, and then tap Save.

6. The next step is to choose the photos that will go into the album. The iPad will show you all your photos. You can tap a photo to choose it, and tap again to de-select it. Your chosen photos have a blue tick on them. You can drag the page up and down as necessary to see all your photos, and can tap the buttons at the top to browse photos by which album they're already in, or by events.

7. Tap Done in the top right.

8. To add photos to an album in future, go into the album and then tap the Use Photo button in the top right and then tap Add Photos.

There's also a Select All button you can use at the top of the screen on the left, to pick all photos. If you want all but a few of them, use the Select All button and then tap those you don't want, to remove the ticks from them.

Note that when you add a photo to an album, it doesn't remove it from the album it was previously in. If you add a photo to a new album, any edits you make to it will be made to the copies of the photo in *both* albums. That's because there's really just one copy of the photo but the albums provide different ways of finding and viewing it.

# Editing your photos on your iPad

When you're viewing a photo, either in the Camera Roll or in the Photos app, there's an Edit button at the top of the screen, right of centre. When you tap that, four new editing options appear at the bottom of the screen:

- **Rotate:** Tap this to rotate the image to the left by 90 degrees. If you need to rotate an image 90 degrees right, you'll have to tap the button three times. Tap Save in the top right to keep your rotated picture.

- **Enhance:** When you tap this button, the iPad will adjust the picture's contrast, colour saturation and other qualities to improve it. You can't control these settings, but if you don't like the iPad's changes, you don't have to keep them. Tap Save in the top right to keep the enhanced version, or tap Cancel in the top left to discard the changes.

- **Red-Eye:** The iPad doesn't have a flash built in, so you're unlikely to have red-eye in photos you take with it. You can fix red-eye in a photo you've copied to the iPad, however, so you could take a photo using your best digital camera or your iPhone and then fix any red-eye using your iPad's larger screen. Tap the Red-Eye button, and then use the pinch gesture to zoom in and tap each eye. The iPad will show you a white ring around the eye when it's worked. If it can't find a red eye to correct, there will be an error message in the bottom left corner. If you correct an eye and then tap it again, the red-eye will be put back. When you've finished, tap the Apply button in the top right, or tap Cancel in the top left to abandon your changes.

- **Crop:** Cropping is used to cut edges off the photo to get rid of distracting detail or improve the composition. To use it, tap the Crop button and a grid will appear (see Figure 11.5). Touch a corner of the grid and drag it, and the size and shape of the grid will change as you move its corner. When you lift your finger, the screen display will adjust to focus on the area inside the grid, which will be staying in your picture. Anything outside the grid is shaded out and will be cut off the picture when you've finished. When you've got the crop roughly right, you can adjust it to fit a particular shape, such as a perfect square or 4x6. To adjust the dimensions, tap Constrain at the bottom of the screen and then tap one of the options. You can also pinch to zoom while cropping. When you've finished, tap Crop in the top right to keep your changes, or Cancel in the top left to discard them.

You can tap Undo in the top left repeatedly to reverse the edits you've made, in order. Tap Revert to Original to discard all your edits.

Take care because any edits you make will overwrite the original picture. The exceptions to this are photos synchronised from your computer using the iTunes software, which cannot be overwritten or deleted on the iPad. If you edit these, a new version of the picture will be saved in the Camera Roll.

**Figure 11.5**

Photos added to the Camera Roll can be copied to other devices using Photo Stream, but be warned: any edits you make on the iPad might not show on other devices or in other software programs. At the time of writing, iPad edits aren't shown in Windows at all when photos are copied to your PC using the iCloud Photo Stream. Before spending too much time editing photos you intend to use on other devices, I recommend you do a quick test to make sure the edits work on your other devices or programs okay.

## Viewing videos on your iPad

If you have shot your own videos using the iPad, you will find them in your Camera Roll album in the Photos app. The videos appear as thumbnails, mixed in among your still photos. When you tap one, the first frame fills the screen; to play it, just tap the Play button in the middle of the screen or in the top left. Across the top of the screen is a control showing different frames from the film. By touching this, you can jump to different parts of the film, and then play or pause using the button in the top left.

When you tap the Use Video button in the top right (this looks the same as the Use Photo button indicated in Figure 11.4), you can email the video or upload it to video-sharing site YouTube, so anyone can see it on the Internet.

## Summary

● The Camera app is used to take photos on iPads with built-in cameras.

● If you allow the camera to use your location, you can view the photos you take with your iPad on a map.

● When taking photos with the iPad, tap the most important part of the picture to focus.

● You use the pinch gesture to zoom the camera.

- To take a picture, put your finger on the Take Picture button on screen, steady the camera and then lift your finger.

- You can also use the physical Volume Up button to take a photo.

- Images and videos created using the iPad go into your Camera Roll album.

- The Photo Booth app that comes with iPads that have built-in cameras enables you to take pictures with special effects applied.

- Even if you don't have an iPad with cameras, you can use your iPad to view your photos.

- The Photos app is used to view photos.

- The Photos app is also used to view videos you've created on the iPad.

- You can start a slideshow of photos from the Photos app, including your choice of musical accompaniment.

- The Picture Frame feature enables your iPad to work as a digital photo frame.

- You can make basic photo edits on the iPad: rotating photos, fixing colours and red-eye, and cropping.

- If you save edits to a photo on your iPad, you will overwrite the original, unless the photo was synchronised from your computer using the iTunes software.

- You can organise your photos in albums for slideshows or to make them easier to find.

# Brain Training

Now that you're an expert on browsing photos and videos with your iPad, and taking them yourself if you have an iPad with cameras, let's try a short quiz.

**1. When taking a photo with the iPad, you can zoom in by:**

(a) Using the pinch gesture

(b) Using the Volume Up button

(c) Using the front camera

(d) Tapping and holding the Take Picture button

**2. The Camera Roll is:**

(a) What happens when you rotate your iPad

(b) The album containing photos you've copied from your camera

(c) The album containing the photos you've taken or images you've made on your iPad

(d) A somewhat dry and crunchy sandwich

**3. To see the videos you've shot on your iPad, you use:**

(a) The Camera app

(b) The Videos app

(c) The Photo Booth app

(d) The Photos app

**4. To zoom the view of a photo you've taken, you can:**

(a) Tap the photo and use the zoom control

(b) Rotate the screen so the photo fills it

(c) Use the pinch gesture to zoom in

(d) Double-tap the photo

**5. To start the Picture Frame feature, you need to:**

(a) Tap its icon on the Home Screen

(b) Tap the flower icon on the lock screen

(c) Tap Picture Frame in the Photos app

(d) Go into the Camera app

## Answers

Q1 – a          Q2 – c          Q3 – d          Q4 – b, c and d          Q5 – b

# Adding and managing apps on your iPad

**Equipment needed:** An iPad with an Internet connection.

**Skills needed:** Experience using the iTunes store (see Chapter 9) is helpful but not essential. Familiarity with gesture controls is helpful (see previous chapters).

So far in this book, you've learned about the many things your iPad can do using the apps that Apple installs on your iPad for you. That's only the start of the story, though. There are thousands of programmers out there, and they're constantly coming up with new apps that allow you to use your iPad in all kinds of imaginative ways. However obscure you think your hobby is, there's bound to be an app for it among the 200,000 apps designed for the iPad.

In this chapter, I'll show you how to download new apps to your iPad, how to remove them and how to organise them. I'll also give you a few pointers to some of the best apps you might want to try out.

There are lots of free apps available, and many people spend more time using apps they've downloaded than the built-in apps. In some ways, this is the most important chapter in this book.

## Downloading apps to your iPad

All the apps you add to your iPad, including the free ones, come through the App Store, which is part of the iTunes store. When you tap the App Store icon on your Home screen, you'll see a screen that looks similar to the iTunes store for music and video (see Chapter 9).

You navigate the App Store like a web page (see Chapter 8). To see more offers, drag the screen up. To jump back to the top, tap the status bar. To find out more about a particular app or offer, tap its artwork. As in the music and video store, you buy and/or download an app by tapping its Price button.

At the bottom of the screen are buttons to take you into different parts of the store (see Figure 12.1). It's worth checking what's new in the Featured section from time to time, because this shows Apple's hand-picked recommendations for the best apps. The Top Charts section shows you the most popular paid and free apps, which is another nice way to uncover some gems. You can also tap the Categories button to see apps organised by categories such as books, business, education, health and fitness, music, lifestyle, news, travel and weather.

> If you go into the Genius section, via the button at the foot of the page, the App Store will recommend new apps for you based on others you've down-loaded. You first need to turn on Genius for apps, and accept the terms and conditions. This is a great way to find new apps you'll like.

You can search for apps using the search box in the top right of the screen. The search results screen has some filters across the top, so you can refine your results to focus on one category, new releases, apps with top ratings and those that are free.

There are three types of app:

- **iPhone apps**: These are apps that were designed for the iPhone and iPod touch, which are pocket-sized devices. Their apps work fine on the iPad, too, but they only use a tiny portion of the screen. When you are using an iPhone app, you can tap the 2x button in the bottom right to enlarge it to fill the screen, but that can make the content appear 'blocky'.

- **iPad apps**: These are designed for your iPad and will make full use of the available screen space. These are sometimes called HD apps (short for high definition), although that doesn't necessarily mean they make full use of the higher quality screen on the third generation iPad. The term was originally used to differentiate iPad apps from those designed for the iPhone's smaller screen.

- **Hybrid apps**: These are designed to work well on both the iPad and the iPhone, so you can use them with confidence on your iPad. If you have an iPhone or iPod touch, you can also use the app on those devices, and it will often have a different screen layout to accommodate the smaller screen size. Hybrid apps are indicated with a tiny + in the top-left corner of the Buy/Download button.

You can filter your search results to show only apps that are designed for the iPad. On the search results page, tap Device at the top and choose iPad. The search on the iPad also prioritises apps designed for the iPad and shows them higher up the screen.

When you find an app you like the sound of, tap its icon to see its information page, which is organised like Figure 12.1. You can drag the page up to see more information, including ratings and reviews from previous customers at the bottom of the screen. You can drag the screenshot left to see more pictures, too. The description is provided by the developer, and some pages will also show information about what's new in the latest version of the app. Tap More on the right to show the description and information about what's new in full.

Most apps work on all the iPad models, but it's worth checking the requirements on the left before downloading, especially if you have a first generation iPad or an iPad 2. iOS is the name of the iPad's software, and you can check which version your iPad has by going into the Settings app, tapping General, and then tapping Software Update. Chapter 2 explains how to update your iPad software if necessary. If you have the Messages and Reminders apps, your iPad has at least iOS 5.0 on it, so it should be able to use any app requiring a lower version number than that.

Some apps are free to download, but enable you to buy additional content from inside the app. These 'in-app purchases' are sometimes used to buy the latest content for a newspaper app or additional characters for a game app. Where an app enables in-app purchases, you can see a chart of the bestsellers on the left. It's worth looking out for this because you can sometimes download a free app only to find it's empty and you have to buy the content to fill it! The app's reviews will normally warn you if this is likely to happen.

Buy/download

Expand description

**Figure 12.1**

App creators sometimes release versions of their apps for free so you can try them before you buy. These are often called 'lite' versions. Tap the Developer Page link in the top right of the page to see other apps by the same developer, which might include a free version of the app you're looking at. Note that the free versions sometimes include adverts that aren't in the paid version. A lot of work goes into making apps, and they've got to make some money somehow!

To download and install an app, tap the Buy/Download button (the button underneath the app's logo that shows its price). The button will go green and then you just need to tap it again to confirm you want to install the app. If the app is a paid app, your credit card will be charged. If you're not already logged in, you'll be prompted to log in using your Apple ID, which is the same one you use for Find my iPad, music downloads and other services Apple provides.

If you haven't previously downloaded any music, video or apps to your iPad, you'll need to verify your payment information before you can proceed, even if the app is free. You'll be shown your account information, and will need to tap beside where it says 'security code' and enter the three-digit security number on the back of your credit card (or the four digits on the front of an American Express card). When you've finished confirming your details, tap Done in the top right of the window.

Once you've confirmed the purchase or free download, the App Store will close and your app will begin to download to your Home screen. You can watch the downloading progress with a bar that goes across the app's icon, or you can use other apps while you wait. When the download has finished, tap the icon to start using your new app.

You can also download apps using the iTunes software on your computer (click on the left to go into the iTunes Store, and then click App Store at the top of the screen) Any apps you download to your computer can be synchronised to your iPad using iTunes (see Chapter 2).

When you run an app for the first time, you might be asked whether you want to allow push notifications. These enable the app to give you new information when you aren't using it, for example by displaying a 'new message' alert on screen or showing you how many messages you have waiting on the app's icon. You can change which apps may use notifications at any time by going into the Settings app and tapping Notifications on the left. See Chapter 7 for a guide to managing notifications on your iPad.

You might also be asked whether you will allow the app to use your location. Some apps, such as a travel app that finds restaurants near you, will need this to work properly. Others can be enhanced by location services, such as photography apps that store the location with each photo you take, so you don't have to remember it. There are privacy implications, though, because an app could, in theory, publish your location on the Internet or use it to target advertising to you (although few do). I recommend that you only give apps permission to use your location if it's necessary for the app to do what you want it to. You can change which apps can use your location by going into the Settings app and tapping Location Services on the left.

Many apps have their own settings available in the Settings app. If you can't get the app to do something you want, check here.

From time to time, the makers of apps update them. The App Store icon on the Home screen shows you how many updates are available for the apps you have installed on your iPad. The number is in a red circle in the top-right corner of the App Store icon. To get your updates, go into the App Store and then tap Updates at the bottom. Updates are usually free, and bring new features to the app. Occasionally, app creators remove features from their apps, too, so read the version information and reviews to make sure the update won't cut off a feature you like.

## Rearranging your apps and web clips

In this section, I'll show you how to organise the apps on your Home screens, but the same ideas apply to web clips (web page bookmarks that you've added to your Home screen, see Chapter 8).

You can have up to 11 Home screens of apps. The Home screen indicator at the bottom of the screen (see Figure 12.2) shows you how many screens there are (each screen is represented by a dot) and which one you're viewing (the dot that is coloured white). To move between the Home screens, flick left and right. This is the same way you brought up the Spotlight search in Chapter 3.

If you're in a Home screen or the Spotlight search, you can press the Home button to go to the first Home screen.

As you've probably noticed by now, when you rotate your iPad, the apps change their position on the screen. In portrait mode, you have five rows of four apps, and in landscape mode, you have four rows of five apps. The apps are arranged in the same sequence in both modes, filling the rows from the top left, but the different lengths of the rows mean that many of your apps will move to a different position on the screen when your rotate the iPad.

## Using your iPad to rearrange your apps

To rearrange the icons on your iPad, go to a Home screen, and tap and hold one of the icons. All the icons will start to jiggle around, which means you're in the mode for arranging icons, as shown in Figure 12.2. Touch an icon and keep your finger on it and it will enlarge. Without lifting your finger, move it across the screen and the app icon will go with it. Move your app to a space near another app and keep it there, and that app will jump out of the way to make room. When you release your finger, your app will drop into that space.

Apps aren't like folders on your desktop computer, which you can put anywhere on the screen, because you can't have empty spaces between apps. Apps are always arranged in rows starting at the top of the screen. You can't add an app to the second row until the first one is filled. If you want to drop an app into the last available space, move the icon across the screen and hold it in the empty space for a moment before lifting your finger. The app will bounce into the next space, just after the last app on the screen.

The shelf at the bottom of the screen is called the 'dock'. The dock has the same icons on every Home screen. There is room for six apps or folders on the dock and you can move the default apps (Safari, Mail, Photos, Music) to a normal Home screen to make room for your own apps on the dock. When the dock is full, if you want to add a new app to the dock, you need to move one of the apps from there to the Home screen above to make room.

Folder

Home
screen
indicator

Dock

**Figure 12.2**

If you put an app directly on top of another app and then release your finger, a new folder is created and opened containing both apps, shown in Figure 12.3. All the other app icons fade into the background, so just the apps inside the folder can be seen clearly. You can enter a name for the folder, rearrange the apps inside it, and leave the folder again by tapping outside of it. To add new apps to the folder, move them onto the folder's icon, hold for a moment and then release your finger. To remove apps from the folder or change its name, tap it when you are in arrangement mode. You can then edit the name box or drag the icons from the folder into the greyed out parts of the Home screen to lift them out of the folder. To delete a folder, simply remove all the items from it. Once you've finished viewing a folder, just tap outside it to go back to the Home screen. Each folder can hold up to 20 apps.

Moving apps to a different Home screen is a tricky manoeuvre. You need to move an icon to the right or left edge of the screen and then hold it there a moment until the next Home screen rolls into view. If you go too far and move off the screen, the app will bounce back into place and you'll have to start again.

To stop arranging icons, press the Home button. The apps will stop jiggling and you can now start apps by tapping their icons in the usual way. To start an app that's inside a folder, first tap the folder to open it and then tap the app's icon.

**Figure 12.3**

## Using iTunes to rearrange your apps

You can also use the iTunes software on your computer to organise the apps on your iPad, which makes it much easier to move apps between different Home screens. Connect your iPad to your computer, and then click Apps at the top of the screen to view the apps pane. A list of the apps you have on your iPad will appear on the left. Tick the box beside any apps you'd like on your iPad and untick the box beside any apps you don't want on your iPad now. You can install them again later if you want to.

On the right, you can arrange where each app appears on your Home screens. You use the large picture of a Home screen to arrange icons, and the smaller pictures underneath it to choose between Home screens. Click a small Home screen picture to choose that Home screen and you'll see its apps in the large Home screen picture. If you want to change an app's position on the screen, click it, hold down the mouse button, drag the app to the space where you want it and then release the mouse button. The other icons will rearrange themselves to make room. To move an app to a different Home screen, click its icon and drag it in a similar way onto the small Home screen box underneath. To start a new Home screen, drag your icon onto the greyed-out box to the right of your choice of Home screens. To make a folder containing apps, use your mouse to drag one app directly on top of another app. Using iTunes is an easier way to organise your apps, but it does mean you have to use your computer to do it.

## Deleting apps and web clips

When you are in arrangement mode, all the apps and web clips you've added to your iPad have an X in the top-left corner. To delete a web clip, tap this X and then confirm you want to delete it. (You can't delete web clips using the iTunes software on your computer.)

If you tap the X in the top-left corner of an app's icon, it will ask you to confirm you want to delete it, before deleting the app and all its data from the iPad. You can download any apps you remove again by going into the App Store and then tapping Purchased at the bottom of the screen.

## Multitasking with apps on your iPad

When you quit an app by pressing the Home button, the iPad keeps a record of the state the app was in when you did that. This means you should see the same documents and information on screen when you return to the app.

There is a quick way to switch between different apps you've recently used. If you press the Home button twice quickly, the Home screen fades out and the Multitasking bar pops up from the bottom of the screen underneath the dock, showing the icons for the apps you used most recently, as you can see in Figure 12.4. Tap one of these icons to go back into it, or flick the bar to the left to see more apps. If you don't want to use one of these apps, tap in the faded-out area or press the Home button to return to your normal Home screen.

Figure 12.4

You can remove apps from the Multitasking bar if you want to. Press the Home button twice to show the list, then tap and hold one of the icons. They will all start to jiggle around. Tap the minus sign in the top left corner of an icon and it will be removed from the list. To finish, tap outside the Multitasking bar or press the Home button.

Flick the Multitasking bar to the right and you can call up brightness, volume and Music app playback controls. There's also a button in the bottom left of this panel to lock the screen orientation. Normally the screen contents adapt to which way up you hold your iPad, but locking the screen orientation stops this.

## Using multitasking gestures

There are also three gestures you can use to switch between different apps and the Home screen:

- Put four or five fingers on the screen and pinch them together to return to the Home screen from any app.

- Put four or five fingers on the screen and drag them up the screen to show the Multitasking bar so you can switch between apps quickly.

- Put four or five fingers on the screen and swipe left or right across the screen to move between apps. This enables you to quickly hop between apps without going through the Home screen or the Multitasking bar.

Try the gesture to move between apps. It really does make it much easier to multitask on the iPad.

## 10 more apps to get you started

Part of the fun of the iPad is exploring the store to find the apps that are perfect for you – the apps on someone's iPad are as much an indicator of their personality as the books they own. But to get you started, here are some suggestions for apps you might want to take a look at. Many of these are free at the time of writing, but prices and specifications change from time to time, so check the store for the latest information.

- **Alltop**: A hand-picked directory of the best websites about a wide range of topics. The app shows you the latest headlines from each site in each subject, and you can easily hop between articles on different websites.

- **BBC iPlayer**: Brings selected BBC TV and radio programmes to your iPad.

- **Cut the Rope**: An addictive puzzle game with cute graphics for the iPad. Try the free lite version first, which includes a tutorial.

- **Draw Something**: Challenge friends or strangers in this game where you take turns drawing something or guessing what your co-player has drawn.

- **Fotopedia Heritage**: 25,000 photographs of all UNESCO World Heritage Sites.

- **GarageBand**: Apple's simple music studio enables you to play an onscreen keyboard, drum kit, guitar and sampler.

- **Guardian Eyewitness**: Every day, a new high-quality reportage photo is downloaded to your iPad, together with a photography tip.

- **iTunes U:** This app delivers free university courses from some of the world's leading universities, including the Open University and Massachusetts Institute of Technology. Courses can include videos, audio recordings and written materials. Subjects are diverse and include creative writing, psychology, law, and computing.

- **Paint Sparkles**: The children in our family loved this app, which gives them animal pictures to colour in. There's a free version with a limited number of pictures to colour in which you can try before deciding whether to buy the full version.

- **Trip Advisor**: A handy app for your holidays. Find restaurants, hotels, and tourist attractions near you and read reviews from other travellers.

If you're a keen gamer, tap the Game Center icon on your Home screen to find games that you can play against your friends over the Internet.

You can find links to these apps (plus suggestions for other apps to try) in the section of my website devoted to this book at **www.sean.co.uk**.

## Summary

- You can enhance your iPad with free and paid apps.

- All apps are downloaded from the App Store, using the App Store app on your iPad or iTunes software on your computer.

- Your iPad can run iPhone apps too, but they only use a small portion of the screen.

- To download an app on your iPad, tap its price in the store.

- Free updates for your apps are available in the App Store, too.

- Push notifications enable apps to give you an alert even when the app isn't running.

- Tap and hold an icon on your Home screen to go into arrangement mode.

- In arrangement mode, you can rearrange your app icons or create folders for your apps.

- You can have up to 11 Home screens of apps.

- Apps on the dock are always visible on screen, whichever Home screen you are viewing.

- To see recently used apps, press the Home button twice quickly.

- The best app on the iPad is whatever turns out to be your favourite. Everyone's different, so explore the store!

# Brain Training

Are you app happy, or appsolutely confused? Try this quick quiz to refresh the key points in this chapter.

**1. The 2x button is used to:**

(a) Download an app again

(b) See the apps you recently used

(c) Enlarge an iPhone app to fill the screen

(d) Cheat by making two moves in the Noughts and Crosses app

**2. Pressing the Home button twice quickly will:**

(a) Go into arrangement mode

(b) Take you to the Spotlight search

(c) Show you recently used apps

(d) Provide quick access to lock the screen orientation

**3. If you drag one app on top of another app in arrangement mode:**

(a) Your iPad creates a new folder containing both apps

(b) Other apps jump out of the way to make room for the app you're dragging

(c) The apps swap places

(d) The app you're dragging jumps to the next free space

**4. If you put four fingers on the screen and pinch them together:**

(a) You'll return to the Home screen

(b) You'll show the Multitasking bar

(c) You'll close the Multitasking bar

(d) You'll enter arrangement mode

**5. To download an app from the App Store on your iPad:**

(a) Tap its artwork

(b) Tap its name

(c) Tap its price

(d) Tap 'More'

## Answers

Q1 – c          Q2 – c and d          Q3 – a          Q4 – a          Q5 – c

# PART V
## Using maps and books on the iPad

Why are so many people reading books about apples these days?

# Finding your way with Maps

**Equipment needed:** An iPad with an Internet connection (Wi-Fi or 4G/3G).

**Skills needed:** Experience of starting apps (see Chapter 2), using the keyboard (see Chapter 3), managing bookmarks (see Chapter 8) and using the Contacts app (see Chapter 4).

If you get lost, your trusty iPad can show you the way. It uses information about the Wi-Fi network or cellular network you're using, plus satellite positioning technology if you have a 4G/3G iPad, to work out where you are.

The Maps app enables you to view street maps, satellite photos, photos of buildings, and traffic jams. It's powered by Google Maps, so if you've used that website it will be familiar to you. The Maps app uses many ideas you've come across in previous chapters, including bookmarks and the pinch gesture (see Chapter 8) and contacts (see Chapter 4).

In this chapter, I'll show you to how to use the app to plot a trip to visit a friend. First, tap the Maps icon on your Home screen or use the Spotlight search to start the app.

To use the Maps app, you need to have an Internet connection.

## Finding where you are on the map

When the Maps app opens, it shows you where it thinks you are, using a blue pin. Around it is a blue ring that tells you how confident the iPad is in its guess: the larger the ring, the less precise the position is. Usually, it's accurate enough for you to find your way around easily. If there is no blue ring, the location should be spot-on.

If you have disabled location services in the Settings app to preserve battery life, you'll need to enable them again to enable the Maps app to find your location. To get an idea of the surrounding area, you can use a couple of gestures you've seen in other apps. You can drag the map around by putting your finger on it and moving it. New bits of the map are downloaded from the Internet as they're needed, so it might take a moment for the new map information to appear. At any time, you can jump back to your current location on the map by tapping the arrow icon, indicated in Figure 13.1.

You can use the pinch gesture you learned in Chapter 8 to zoom in and out. You can even zoom all the way out to see where you are on a global map. Suddenly, the world doesn't seem so small after all.

A double-tap will zoom in too, and you can double-tap repeatedly to keep enlarging the map until you can't zoom any further. A single tap with two fingers zooms out.

This app offers four different types of map: Standard (a street map), Satellite (which shows satellite photographs), Hybrid (which shows satellite photos with roads overlaid on top) and Terrain (which uses colour to indicate the height of the land). To change between them, tap in the bottom right of the screen to 'peel back' the map to reveal the options (see Figure 13.2). You can also switch on the Traffic option, which colour codes some roads to show you whether the traffic is currently flowing (green), slow (yellow) or jammed (red). If you have a printer that supports AirPrint, you can print maps and directions in these options too. They come out in an ideal format for reading in the car (from the passenger seat).

Arrow          Search box

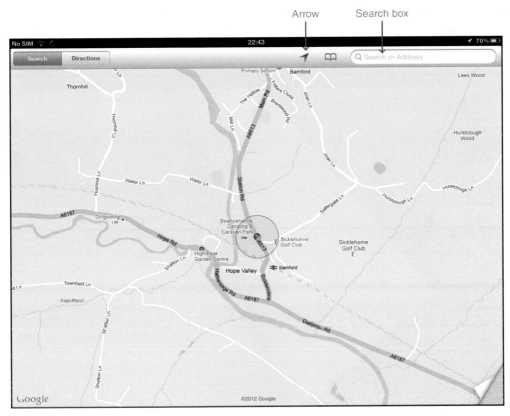

©2012 Google.

**Figure 13.1**

The iPad enables you to drop a pin on the map as a place marker. Just tap and hold on the map, and a purple pin will drop from the sky at that point. If you tap the Drop Pin button, which appears when you tap in the bottom right of the map, a pin is placed in the middle of the map. You can only have one dropped pin at a time, so it's better to create a bookmark for places you want to remember, as you'll discover later in this chapter.

The iPad has a compass built in to it, too. Tap the Arrow icon so it shows your current location and is coloured purple, and then tap it again. To calibrate the compass, you might need to wave the iPad around in the air in a figure of eight pattern (seriously – I'm not making this up!). You'll see instructions on screen if you need to do this. When the compass is active, you'll see a North indicator in the top right of the map, and you can rotate the iPad to orientate it towards North. You can use the pinch gesture to zoom, but if you tap or drag the map, the compass will turn off. The Arrow icon changes its appearance when the compass is active and you can tap it again to turn the compass off.

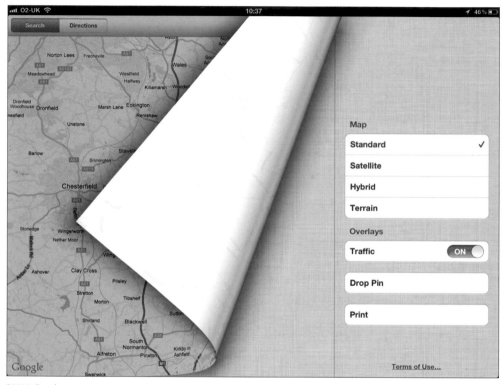

©2012 Google.

**Figure 13.2**

See if you can find a satellite photo of your house, or wherever you are at the moment. Start by finding your current location, switch the view to satellite, and then zoom in.

# Getting directions to a friend's house

You can find any place in the world by typing a place or business name into the Search box in the top right of the screen (shown in Figure 13.1). Try 'Eiffel Tower' and 'Downing Street', for example. If you enter a street name with more than one match, the app will ask you which one you want before displaying it.

You can also use the addresses in the Contacts app. Here's how you get directions to a friend's house:

1. Tap the Bookmarks icon. This looks the same as it does in Safari and is indicated in Figure 13.3.

2. A menu will open (see Figure 13.3). If your contacts aren't showing, tap Contacts in the bottom right of the menu.

3. Use the Search box at the top of the menu, or scroll the alphabetically sorted list to find your friend and then tap his or her name.

4. The map moves to your friend's house and a red pin is dropped with their name above it, as you can see for Humphrey Appleby in Figure 13.3.

Once you've found your friend's house, you can zoom in. If there's an icon of a person next to their name above their pin, then you can tap it to see a street view of their road, which will look similar to the one in Figure 13.4. This shows you panoramic photos that have been taken of the street by one of Google's roving cars, tricycles or (more rarely) snowmobiles. Street names appear down the middle of the roads, and you can tap the arrows on them to move along the street. You can pinch to zoom or touch the screen and move your finger around to spin the view through 360 degrees or look up and down. This is a great way to check for landmarks on the route before you leave, which can help you get your bearings when you get there. If your friend says you need to take the lane after the post office, for example, you can do a recce on the iPad first and more easily recognise it while you're driving along at 30mph. Be warned, though, that Google's photos might have been taken some years ago, and things might have changed a bit since then. When you've finished, tap the circle with the map in it at the bottom right to go back to the map.

**Figure 13.3**

If you tap the information icon on the label on someone's pin, it will show you their address and allow you to choose whether you want directions to their house or from their house. If you tap for directions to their house, a blue line is drawn on the map for each suggested driving route. You tap a route to select it, and the blue bar at the bottom of the screen shows the estimated distance and journey time for your chosen route. The selected route is shown with a thick blue line, but the semi-transparent line used for the other routes can be hard to differentiate from motorways and rivers. One tip is that most routes merge at the start and end of the journey, so this part of the route will always be shown with a highly visible thick blue line. You can tap this shared part of the journey to switch between selecting the alternative routes.

©2009 Google.

**Figure 13.4**

The blue bar at the bottom of the screen also has three icons for travelling by car, by public transport and on foot. Tap your preferred mode of transport, and you'll see the estimated travel time. Tap the Start button in the blue bar to begin your directions.

If you're using public transport, tap the clock icon in the blue bar (where available) to see the timetable. It's a good idea to double check with the transport operator directly because schedules are subject to change and these changes might not be reflected in the iPad app.

You can advance through the directions in the blue bar one at a time by tapping the Next and Previous buttons shown in Figure 13.5. You can also tap the List button (shown in Figure 13.5) to see all your instructions in a list, as in Figure 13.6. You can scroll this list and tap the steps in it to see them illustrated on the map. To hide the list again, tap the button indicated in Figure 13.6.

**Figure 13.5**

Hopefully, that will help your visit go smoothly! If you fancy an excursion with the friends you're visiting or you want to plan other routes, you can get directions between any two places. Tap Directions in the top left first, if necessary, and then enter the start and end places in the boxes in the top right (see Figure 13.6). Both will give you the option to choose from places you've recently searched for or dropped pins on. The button between the two boxes is used to reverse them, so that you can see directions for your return trip.

If there's a place you want to remember, tap and hold your finger on the map and a pin will drop there. Like the pins your contacts have, this has an Information button you can use for plotting routes, and a Street View button. You can only have one dropped pin at a time, so if you want to keep a record of an address, you need to create a bookmark for it. Tap the pin's Information button and then tap Add to Bookmarks. You enter a name for the bookmark, and then tap Save. You can see your bookmarks by tapping the Bookmarks button (see Figure 13.3) and then tapping Bookmarks in the bottom left of the menu that opens.

When you've finished with your directions, you can bring back the Search box again by tapping Search in the top left (see Figure 13.6). If your journey has worked up a thirst, try searching for café (or pub!) to see all the refreshment stops on the map.

The Bookmarks menu can also show you Recents, the places and directions you last searched for, and the locations where you have dropped pins.

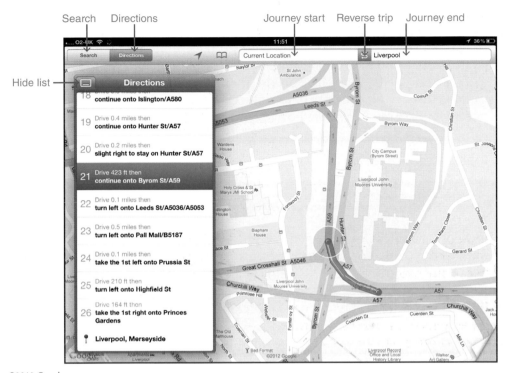

©2012 Google.

**Figure 13.6**

# Using Maps to update your address book

The Maps app can help you to keep your address book updated, and sometimes it's quicker to find an address in Maps than to type it in – especially if you're already there.

Here's how. When you're at a friend's house, connect using 4G/3G or ask your friend if you can use their Wi-Fi. In the Maps app, tap the arrow to find your current location, tap the blue pin, tap the Information button in the label that opens and then choose Add to Contacts. You can then add the address of where you are to an existing or new contact. Don't forget to edit the house number and post code to make sure they're accurate, using the techniques you learned in Chapter 3.

You can also add addresses using dropped pins, from the comfort of your home. Find an address on the map, tap and hold, and then tap the Information button on the label that opens. The iPad will invite you to add that address to a new or existing contact. You can also use the Information button on any businesses shown on the map and add them to your contacts too.

## Summary

● To use Maps on your iPad, you need to have an Internet connection.

● To find your location on the map, you need to have location services enabled.

● Tap the Arrow icon to see your current location. Tap it again to turn the compass on.

● The blue pin shows you where you are on the map.

● You can drag the map and double-tap or pinch to zoom.

● To choose the map type and turn on traffic settings, tap in the bottom right of the map.

● Use the Search box to search for a place by name or a type of business.

● Tap and hold on the map to drop a pin.

● Tap the Bookmarks button to find your bookmarks and contacts on the map.

● Tap the Information button on a pin's label to plot a route to or from there, create a bookmark or add an address to a contact.

# Brain training

Find out if you've mastered Maps with this short quiz.

**1. Using the Maps app, you might be able to see:**

    a) A friend's house, as seen from a taxi

    b) Your house, as viewed from space

    c) The Houses of Parliament, as seen from inside

    d) The terrain of the Alps

**2. A yellow line along a road on the map means:**

    a) It's a dirt track

    b) The road is closed

    c) Traffic is moving slowly

    d) There's been a custard spillage following a lorry accident

**3. To see what a shop's front door looks like:**

    a) Drop a pin and tap the Information button on its label

    b) Drop a pin and tap the person icon on its label

    c) Use the pinch gesture to zoom in

    d) Change the map view to Satellite

**4. To choose between suggested routes:**

    a) Tap the Next button

    b) Tap the Start button

    c) Tap the route lines on the map

    d) Tap the Directions button

**5. To go back to some directions you recently searched for:**

    a) Tap the Previous button

    b) Tap the Bookmarks button

    c) Tap Directions

    d) Tap Reverse Trip

## Answers

**Q1** – a, b and d      **Q2** – c      **Q3** – b      **Q4** – c      **Q5** – b

**Equipment needed:** An iPad with an Internet connection.

**Skills needed:** Experience installing apps (see Chapter 12). Experience using the iTunes store (see Chapter 9) is helpful but not essential.

If you're an avid reader, you've probably noticed the publishing revolution that has taken place in the last few years: the ebook. This is a digital version of a book that has been created for reading on dedicated ebook reading devices like Amazon's Kindle, or on multipurpose devices like your iPad.

Although more people still read paper books than ebooks, it tends to be the most passionate readers who have gone digital. Why? It's so convenient. You can buy a book anywhere you can get an Internet connection and start reading in a minute or two. In the summer, you can take thirty books on holiday without paying for excess baggage. You can increase the text size and enlarge photos, search an ebook for particular words or names, and can add bookmarks. Sometimes the content is enhanced with videos, audio recordings, or interactive animations.

Apple has an ebook reading app called iBooks, which is supported by its own book store. There's also a part of the App Store for magazines called Newsstand, and you can use a Kindle app to read books from Amazon's store too. In this chapter, I'll introduce you to the joy of reading on your iPad.

Alaska Airlines has ditched the heavy airline manuals pilots used to carry around in favour of the iPad. Instead of carrying 11kg of paper onto the plane, each pilot has a company-issued iPad with 41 flight, systems and performance manuals on it.

## Installing iBooks on your iPad

Although Newsstand comes pre-installed on your iPad, you will have to go to the App Store and download iBooks for free (see Chapter 12 for a guide to finding and downloading apps). While you're there, you might want to download the Kindle app too. This enables you to read ebooks from Amazon's store. Having both apps gives you a wider choice of books and enables you to shop for the keenest price.

The apps are free, but you'll have to pay to download many of the books. Publishers do sometimes make ebooks available for free or cheaper than printed books, so it's worth browsing your favourite authors and genres to see what's on offer. Classic works of literature are often available for free download because they're out of copyright.

When you first start the app, it will ask if you want to sync your bookmarks, notes and collections between devices. If you plan to use iBooks on a number of different devices, this helps you to keep all your information synchronised across them, so that if you stopped reading your latest mystery on page 57, you can open up to the same spot on any device. You can change your mind by turning off this option in the Settings app later if you need to.

## Downloading books using iBooks

When the app starts, you'll see an empty bookshelf. When you have some books, it'll look more like the shelf in Figure 14.1. To download your first books, tap Store in the top left of the screen and you'll enter the book store, which looks and feels the same as the App Store (see Chapter 12) and the iTunes music store (see Chapter 9). As with apps and music, you tap the Price button to buy a book. You download a free ebook by tapping the Free button that replaces its price. If you want to weigh up a book before buying it, tap the Get Sample button.

When you buy or download a book for free, you're taken back to your bookshelf automatically. If you decide to leave the store without getting a new book, tap Library in the top left to return to your bookshelf.

To the store

Change library view

**Figure 14.1**

When you have too many books to fit on the screen, you can scroll your bookshelf by dragging it up. You can also drag down to reveal a search box above the top shelf, so you can quickly find a specific title. I wish they'd invent something similar that works in my town library.

# Reading books using iBooks

To start reading a book, tap its cover in your library on your bookshelf. You can read books in portrait (where the pictures might be larger) or landscape orientation (which feels more like a real book).

> You can often double-tap a picture to enlarge it and then use the pinch gesture on it to zoom in further. When you've finished, tap the picture and then tap Done in the top right.

To turn to the next page, put your finger on the right of the screen and flick it left. To go back a page, put your finger on the left of the screen and flick it right. You can also slide the page chooser along the bottom of the screen.

Figure 14.2 shows iBooks in action, with its controls labelled.

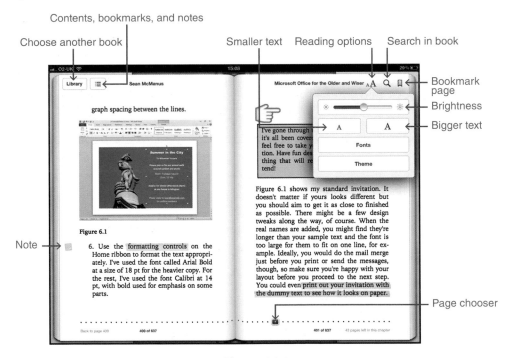

**Figure 14.2**

There's some clever stuff you can do with a digital book (ebook) that you can't do with a real book. Double tap a word, for example, and you can adjust the grab points to select text (see Chapter 3). There are a number of things you can do to selected text: have it spoken aloud to you, copy it for pasting into other apps like Notes, search for it elsewhere in the book, look it up in the dictionary, highlight it using one of five colours, or add a note about it.

Unlike when you scribble comments in the margin of a printed book, you can quickly see all your notes in one place by going to the Bookmarks page for your ebook. When you're reading a book, the notes appear in the margin. Just tap them to enlarge them, and tap outside them to hide them again. To see your notes and bookmarks, tap in the top left (see Figure 14.2).

If you find the iBooks controls distracting, you can tap the page to hide them. Tap again to bring them back when you need them.

If you struggle to read small print, you can change the text size. Just tap where indicated in Figure 14.2 to open the reading options. Then tap the Bigger Text button until you can read comfortably. You can also change the text style used (the font), and the theme to something easier on the eyes. There is a Sepia theme if you find the white pages too dazzling, and a Night theme which uses white text on a black background, so there's less light glaring at you when you're reading in the dark.

Books can include links, too. For example, if you tap an entry in the table of contents, you'll jump to the relevant section of the book. You can see the table of contents by tapping the button in the top left indicated in Figure 14.2. You can also tap a website link to open its web page in Safari.

When you're reading a free sample of a book, there is a Buy button in the top-left corner. Tap that to skip to the last page in the sample, where there is a price button you can tap to buy.

In the top right you'll find two basic but useful controls: there's a Bookmark button, which you can use to mark a page that you're interested in coming back to later. Tap the button in the top left (shown in Figure 14.2) to see all your bookmarked pages at a glance. There's also a search option in the top right (see Figure 14.2), so you can scan the whole book for a particular word or phrase.

When you've finished reading, tap Library in the top left to return to your bookshelves.

There are lots of great free books available, so why not see what you can find? At the time of writing, you can get free books from Beatrix Potter, Charles Dickens, HG Wells and many more.

For a glimpse into the future of storytelling, take a look at the free ebook based on *Yellow Submarine*, the film by The Beatles. This is one of Apple's new interactive books, with sound effects, video and animations integrated. Apple promises many more interactive books in future, and a number of interactive textbooks are already available in the US. Note that interactive books often work differently, and many of the tips in this section won't work for them.

## Using the Amazon Kindle app

If you've already got iBooks, why would you want Amazon's rival ebook app too? Firstly, its books are sometimes cheaper than Apple's, and secondly, you can read the books you buy from Amazon on lots of other devices too, including the Kindle. By comparison, books bought on iBooks can only be read on compatible Apple devices.

The main gotcha with the Kindle app is that there's no store built in and no hint about where you find it. To buy content or order free content, you have to visit the Amazon website at **www.amazon.co.uk** using your web browser (see Chapter 8). Any orders you make are then sent to your Kindle app.

## Using Newsstand to buy magazines

There is also a part of the App Store you can use to find newspapers and magazines for your iPad, called Newsstand. It has a special folder on your Home screen. When you tap the folder, which looks just like an app icon, it will show you the magazines you have downloaded (if any) and will give you a Store button you can tap to find more. Typically, you download an app that's like a catalogue of issues, and you can then choose to buy individual issues or subscribe to get each issue when it comes out. Because each publication has created its own app, there's a lot of variance in the designs, much more so than with ebooks.

## Summary

- To read books on your iPad, you can install Apple's iBooks app.

- The apps and many classic books are free, but you'll have to pay for other content.

- You can synchronise your iBooks bookmarks, notes and collections between different devices.

- Tap Store in the top left of the iBooks app to browse and download books, both free and paid.

- You can read books in portrait or landscape modes.

- Just flick the page to turn it.

- If you select text, you can copy it, look it up in the dictionary, highlight it or add a note to it.

- Tap in the top left to see the table of contents, bookmarks and notes.

- You can adjust the text style and size to your preference, and can change the colour theme to something that's easier on the eyes too.

- You can also install Amazon's rival Kindle app, so you can read ebooks bought at Amazon's website on the iPad too.

- Newsstand is used to find apps based on magazines and newspapers.

# Brain Training

It's the end of this book, but I hope this chapter has helped you to discover your next read. Let's finish up as usual with a quiz.

**1. To find a free book to read in iBooks, you have to:**

   a) Tap Library

   b) Tap Store

   c) Use Newsstand

   d) Use the Kindle app

**2. To see a picture in a book more clearly, you can:**

   a) Tap the picture

   b) Double tap the picture

   c) Rotate your iPad

   d) Squint

**3. If you spot an interesting word in a book and double tap it, you can:**

   a) Find out what it means

   b) Change its text colour

   c) Find out where else in the book it appears

   d) Email your friends about it

**4. If you select text in iBooks, you can:**

   a) Have it read aloud

   b) Enlarge it

   c) Add a bookmark

   d) Add a note to it

**5. To buy books to read in the Kindle app, you have to:**

   a) Tap the Store button

   b) Go into the Kindle app

   c) Visit the Amazon website in your browser

   d) Buy a Kindle reader device

## Answers

Q1 – b    Q2 – b and c    Q3 – a and c    Q4 – a and d    Q5 – c

# Glossary

**4G or 3G** A mobile Internet connection that works in a similar way to a mobile phone connection. You need to pay a subscription to use 4G or 3G and have a 4G or 3G signal available wherever you are when you want to use it. The signal is available most places in urban areas, most of the time. iPads that support 4G or 3G cost more. 4G is only supported by third-generation iPads and networks are not currently available in the UK, but the iPad will use the best signal available (typically 3G in the UK).

**app** Short for 'application', this is a program on your iPad, such as Notes or Mail. The iPad comes with many apps and you can download additional paid and free apps from the App Store.

**App Store** Apple's App Store enables you to download new apps for your iPad, many of which are free. You can access it through the App Store icon on your iPad's Home screen or by using the iTunes software on your computer.

**Apple ID** You use your personal Apple ID to access various services provided by Apple, including FaceTime, Find my iPad, the iTunes store for buying music and video, and the App Store. Your ID is a combination of your email address and a password you set up when you first create your Apple ID.

**bookmark** Bookmarks are used to keep a note of web pages, ebook pages or map locations you might want to refer back to later.

**Contacts** The Contacts app provides a single place to store information about your friends, which is then shared with the Mail, Maps and FaceTime apps. This ensures those apps have postal addresses, phone numbers and email addresses available to use whenever they're needed.

**dock** The dock is the shelf at the bottom of the Home screen showing several apps. The dock's apps are the same on all your Home screens, so it's used to make sure you can always quickly find the most important apps. A dock is also a device you can buy for propping up your iPad while it is connected to your computer or for connecting it to a keyboard.

**double-tap** To briefly touch something on the screen twice in quick succession.

**drag** A gesture used to scroll around the screen so you can see different content on it. Touch the screen and move your finger up, down, left or right. It is used, for example, if a web page spills off the bottom of the screen and you need to drag the web page up to see more.

**ebook** An ebook is an 'electronic book', a book you can read on your iPad or another electronic device.

**FaceTime** Apple's app for video conferencing. This is only provided on iPads that have built-in cameras.

**flick** A gesture for quickly moving through content. Touch the screen and move your finger left, right, up or down quickly, lifting your finger part-way through.

**gestures** Ways to control the iPad by touching its screen in different ways, such as by briefly touching an icon (tapping it) or by moving your fingers closer together or further apart while they're on the screen's surface (the pinch gesture).

**high definition (HD)** A term for high quality video. Also sometimes used to indicate apps that are designed for the iPad's large screen.

**Home button** The round button on the front of the iPad. Press it to exit apps and return to the Home screen.

**Home screens** The screens full of app icons that enable you to choose which app you'd like to use next.

**iBooks** iBooks is Apple's app for downloading, browsing and reading ebooks on your iPad. You can also use iBooks to read PDF files. You can download the app for free from the App Store.

**iCloud** iCloud is Apple's service for storing your files on its computers in its vast data centre, and making them available to you over the Internet. iCloud can be used for copying content between your devices and for backing up your iPad.

**icon** A small picture used to represent an app on the Home screen. Tap an app's icon to start the app. An icon can also be a symbol inside an app that's used as a button, such as the magnifying glass you tap to search in iBooks.

**iMessage** iMessage is Apple's service for sending instant messages between people using iPads, iPhones or other Apple devices.

**iPhone** Apple's mobile phone, which also runs apps but has a much smaller screen than the iPad. You can use iPhone apps on your iPad, but they only use a small part of the screen by default and can become 'blocky' when you enlarge them.

**iPod** Apple makes a range of music and video players called iPods, including the iPod touch, which can run apps but has a much smaller screen than the iPad.

**iTunes** This word is commonly used to refer to two different things. The iTunes software runs on your computer and is used to manage your iPad and the content on it. The iTunes store is used to buy and download music, video and other content. It is accessed on your iPad by tapping the iTunes icon on the Home screen. You can also access the iTunes store on your computer using the iTunes software.

**iTunes Match** iTunes Match is a subscription service for people with music collections on their computers. It enables you to download and play all your music on your iPad.

**iTunes U** Short for iTunes University, this provides free educational programmes for download from the iTunes store. You can access these using the free iTunes U app, which you'll need to download from the App Store.

**landscape** When you use your iPad in landscape orientation it means it is wider than it is tall, like a painting of a landscape.

**lock** When your iPad is locked, the screen is off and it doesn't respond to your touch. It can continue to play music. To unlock the iPad, press the Home button and slide the onscreen switch. Alternatively, open your iPad's smart cover if it has one.

**Notification Centre** The Notification Centre provides a single panel you can use to see recent alerts from all your apps in one place. You reveal it by dragging down from the top of the screen.

**pinch** A gesture used for enlarging content on screen (zooming in) or reducing its size (zooming out). Put two fingers on the screen and move them further apart to zoom in. Close your fingers together to zoom out again.

**podcast** A podcast is a free video or audio programme you can download using the iTunes store. Lots of radio stations make their programmes available as podcasts, but anyone can publish a podcast so there are lots of inventive amateur productions available too.

**portrait** When you use your iPad in portrait orientation it means it is taller than it is wide, like a portrait painting.

**Sleep/Wake button** This is the button on your iPad that is used to lock your iPad or switch it off. If you hold your iPad with the round Home button at the bottom, the Sleep/Wake button is in the top right corner.

**Spotlight search** The search built into the iPad that can be used to find notes, emails, contacts, videos and audio content stored on your iPad.

**status bar** The black bar across the top of the iPad's screen, which shows the time and the status of the battery and Internet connection. In many apps, you can tap the status bar to jump to the top of the page content.

**synchronising** When you connect your iPad to your computer, content is copied between them both. Your contacts and web browser bookmarks, for example, will be synchronised (synched) so the same information is stored on both your iPad and your computer. You can also choose which audio, video, podcasts, photos and other content are copied from your computer to your iPad. Any content you create or download on your iPad is automatically backed up to your computer when you connect to it. You can synchronise with your computer using Wi-Fi instead of physically connecting it to your iPad, or you can use iCloud so that you don't need to connect your iPad to your computer at all.

**tap** A gesture where you briefly touch something on the screen (or tap it). It is used to start apps by tapping their icons, to select content by tapping its summary (in Notes or Mail), and to press buttons on the screen.

**tap and hold** A gesture where you touch something on the screen and keep your finger on it. You tap and hold an image or a link in the web browser to open additional options, and tap and hold an app icon on the Home screen to enter arrangement mode, for example.

**touchscreen** The screen on the iPad. It not only displays information but also recognises where and when you touch it, so that you can control the iPad.

**unlock** When your iPad is locked, it does not respond to your touch and the screen is off. To unlock your iPad, press the Home button and slide the slider to the right.

**wallpaper** The image that appears behind your icons on your Home screens. You can change your wallpaper in the Settings app.

**web browser** The program used to view and interact with web pages. On the iPad, this is the Safari app.

**web clip** A bookmark for a web page, which appears on your Home screen like an app icon.

**Wi-Fi** A wireless Internet connection that you can use on your iPad to access the Internet, the App Store and the iTunes music and video store. You can set up your own Wi-Fi at home, and it is also often provided at cafés, holiday resorts, and hotels. Wi-Fi only works in a relatively small area, around the Wi-Fi hotspot.

**YouTube** A website that anyone can use to publish and view videos. On your iPad, the YouTube app enables you to search and view videos from the YouTube website. YouTube is owned by Google.

# Index

## A

ABC format, 62
ABC key, 62
accent marks, 60, 138
Accept button (FaceTime app), 122
Accessibility button, 33, 56
Accessibility options, 33, 65, 67, 140
accessories, 15
Add Bookmark, 150–151
Add to Contacts button (Maps app), 241
Add to Favourites (FaceTime app), 119
Add to Home Screen (bookmarks), 151
Add to Home Screen (web clips), 151
Add to Reading List (bookmarks), 151
Add to Reading List option (website links), 147
adding
  bookmarks, 150–151
  CDs, 172–174
  a contact (FaceTime app), 117–118
  Contacts app, 86
  Contacts with keyboard, 87
  email sender as contact, 107
  Home screen, 75, 151, 222
  notes, 71
  photo to contact details, 88

address book, 41, 83–85, 241–242
Adobe, 205
advertised device capacity, 9
adverts, 135, 155–156, 220, 222
Airplane mode, 31
AirPrint, 72, 235
Album browser control (Photos app), 207
Albums button (Photos app), 206, 210
albums by same artist, 168
Albums view (Music app), 180, 182–183, 185
alerts
  events, 90
  iMessage, 126
  Messages app, 132
  push notifications, 221
  Reminders app, 55, 77
  ringtones, 86
  sounds, 77, 119, 122, 132
All Imported folder (Photos app), 206
Alltop app, 228
Amazon, 14, 175, 245, 246, 250
analysing music collection, 174–175, 187
AOL, 96–98
Aperture, 43, 44

apostrophe, 61, 62
app recommendations from Apple, 218
App Store, 3, 165, 218, 221–222,
        226, 253
App Store app, 25
Apple data plans and providers, 12
Apple ID, 22–25, 95, 116–117, 126,
        174, 221, 253
Apple stores, 13–14
Apple supportive services, 3
Apple's reputation, 3
apps
    about, 2, 3, 9, 39–40, 217–227, 253
    Calendar, 25, 88–90
    Camera, 25, 200–203, 205
    Contacts, 25, 83, 85–90, 122,
        171–172, 253
    Cut the Rope app, 228
    Draw Something app, 228
    FaceTime, 22, 25, 36, 86,
        116–122, 254
    Game Center, 25, 228
    GarageBand, 228
    Guardian Eyewitness, 228
    iBooks, 245–250, 254
    iTunes, 25, 173
    Kindle, 246, 250
    Mail, 25, 101, 105–106, 154
    Maps, 25, 234–235, 237, 240, 242
    Messages, 47, 125–126, 130–132
    Music, 25, 180
    Notes, 25, 71–75, 97
    Photo Booth, 25, 203–204
    Photos, 25, 188, 206–213
    Reminders, 25, 55, 75–77
    Settings, 25, 38
    Trip Advisor, 228
    YouTube, 25, 135, 155, 188, 190,
        191–194, 257

apps arrangement, 223
apps folders, 224, 225
The Archers, 166
Archive email folder, 108
archiving email, 107
arranging bookmark folders, 152–153
Arrow icon, 234, 235, 236
Artists view (Music app), 180, 182, 185
artwork
    albums, 167, 170, 182, 184
    app or offer, 218
    films, 168, 171, 189–190
    podcasts, 170
    songs, 183
    TV shows, 168, 171, 189–190
AssistiveTouch feature, 34
attachments, to email, 108
audio content, 34, 108, 166, 170,
        180–183, 187–188
audiobooks. See ebooks
Audiobooks option
    iTunes store, 166
    Music app, 187
Auto-Brightness, 34
automatic downloads, 44
Auto-text, 34, 35, 56, 64–66, 104
A-Z index, 171, 172

**B**

Back button
    browsing, 144
    Music app, 181, 182
    Videos app, 190
back camera, 19, 121, 200, 201, 202
Back control (Photos app), 207
backing up, 22, 42–46
banner, 131. See also alerts

'barrel roll' control, 76–77, 88–89
battery, 2, 17, 48–49, 111
BBC, 166
BBC iPlayer, 194, 228
Bcc (blind copy), 103
Bigger Text button (iBooks app), 249
BIU (bold, italic and underlined
　　formatting), 104
blue speech bubbles, 128
bold formatting, 55, 104
Bolt Beranek and Newman (technology
　　company), 94
book icon, 149
Bookmark button (iBooks app), 249–250
bookmark folders, 149–150, 152–153
bookmarks, 148–153, 249, 253
Bookmarks Bar, 149–150
Bookmarks button, 149
Bookmark/share button, 150, 152, 155
books, 9, 39–40, 246–247
bookshelf, 246–248
brackets, 62
brightness control, 227
Brightness setting, 34
browsing
　　Contacts, 84–86, 102
　　Internet, 135–136
　　iTunes store, 164–167
　　multiple websites, 145–148
　　Music app, 180
Bulk Mail email folder, 108
bullet point, 61
buttons
　　Accept (FaceTime app), 122
　　Accessibility, 33, 56
　　Add to Contacts (Maps app), 241
　　Albums (Photos app), 206, 210
　　Back (browsing), 144
　　Back (Music app), 181, 182

Back (Videos app), 190
Bigger Text (iBooks app), 249
Bookmark (iBooks app), 249–250
Bookmarks, 149
Bookmark/share, 150, 152, 155
Buy (iBooks app), 249
Buy Album (iTunes store), 167
Buy Song (iTunes store), 167
Buy/Download (apps), 221
Categories (App Store), 218
Chapters (Videos app), 190
Check for Update (iTunes
　　software), 47
Crop (Photos app), 211
Decline (FaceTime app), 122
Delete (iMessage), 128
Downloads (iTunes store), 169
Drop Pin (Maps app), 235
Edit (FaceTime app), 119
End Call (FaceTime app), 121
Enhance (Photos app), 211
Forward (browsing), 144
Forward (iMessage), 128
Forward (Music app), 181, 182
Forward (Videos app), 190
Free (iBooks app), 246
Free (iTunes store), 169, 170
Get More Episodes (Videos app), 190
Get Sample (iBooks app), 246
Home, 18, 254
IMAP, 99–100
International Keyboards, 128
Library (iBooks app), 247, 250
Mailboxes (Mail app), 108–109
Mute (FaceTime app), 120
New Album (Photos app), 210
Not On This iPad, 171
Pause/Play (Music app),
　　180–182

buttons *(continued)*
  Places (Photos app), 205
  Playlists (Music app), 186
  Play/Pause (Videos app), 190
  POP, 99–100
  Price (iBooks app), 246
  radio buttons, 145
  Record (Videos app), 203
  red buttons, 153, 186
  Red-Eye (Photos app), 211
  Review Shots (Camera app), 202
  Rotate (Photos app), 211
  Select All (Photos app), 210
  Share Contact (Contacts app),
    84, 86
  Show songs on this album
    (Music app), 184
  Silent, 19
  Sleep/Wake, 19, 26, 27, 256
  Slideshow (Photos app), 208
  Street View (Maps app), 240
  Subscribe (iTunes store), 170
  Swap Cameras (Camera app), 201
  Take Picture (Camera app), 202
  Update Mailbox (date), 111
  Volume, 19
  Volume Up (Camera app), 202
Buy Album button (iTunes store), 167
Buy button (iBooks app), 249
Buy Song button (iTunes store), 167
Buy/Download button (apps), 221
buying music/video from iTunes,
  167–169

**C**

cables, 37, 38, 48
calendar (Reminders app), 77
Calendar app, 25, 88–90

calling up
  brightness, 227
  Music app playback controls, 227
  volume control, 227
Camera app, 25, 200–203, 205
Camera Connection Kit, 205
Camera Roll album, 202–203, 207,
  211–213
Camera Roll folder, 206
cameras, 8, 19, 120, 199–202
cancelling email message, 104
Capacity graph, 41
capitalisation, 59
Cash, Johnny, 164
Categories button (App Store), 218
Cc (courtesy copy), 103
CDs, 164, 172–175
centring keyboard, 129
changing screen orientation, 26
Channel 4's 4oD, 194
Chapman, John (Johnny Appleseed), 97
Chapters button (Videos app), 190
charging battery, 17, 48
Check for Update button (iTunes
    software), 47
checkbox, 145
choosing to use iCloud service, 24
cleaning iPad, 50
Close artwork view button
    (Music app), 184
closing web page, 146
commas, 59
compass feature, 235–236
Composers view (Music app), 184, 185
Contacts app, 25, 83, 85–90, 122,
    171–172, 253
content restrictions, 36
conventions for Contacts app, 87
copy feature, 67–69, 104
Copy options (website links), 147

copying
    CDs, 164, 174
    info between computer and iPad, 17, 37
    music, 164, 174
    photos, 206
credit cards, 22–23, 146, 167–168, 221
Crop button (Photos app), 211
cross icon, 138
currency symbols, 61, 62
cursor, 66–67, 69
cut feature, 67–69, 104
Cut the Rope app, 228

**D**

data collection by Apple, 24, 25
data defined, 12
data plans and providers from Apple, 12
data roaming feature, 32
Decline button (FaceTime app), 122
default apps, 223
Define feature, 70
Delete button (iMessage), 128
Delete photo control (Photos app), 207
deleting
    apps, 226
    bookmark folders, 153
    bookmarks, 153
    email, 107, 109
    notes, 71
    sections (Contacts app), 87
    web clips, 226
Desert Island Discs, 166
Diagnostics section, 25
Dickens, Charles, 250
dictation feature, 8, 24, 63, 127
dictionary, 35, 50, 69–70, 155, 249
dissolve (slideshow special effect), 208

DIY jobs in Notes app, 72
Do nothing option (website links), 147
dock, 25, 101, 223, 254
dock connector, 19, 38, 48
Documents & Data app, 43
domain extensions, 138
.com key, 138
double-tap gesture, 254
downloading
    from App Store, 221, 226
    apps, 218–222
    automatically, 44
    books, 246–247
    email, 110–111
    iBooks app, 246
    with iCloud service, 10
    iTunes app, 221
    from iTunes store, 169–170
    music, 168–172, 174
    podcasts, 40
    software, 37
    TV shows, 168
    video, 168–172
Downloads button (iTunes store), 169
Downloads options (iTunes store), 166
Drafts email folder, 108
drag gesture, 254
Draw Something app, 228
Drop Pin button (Maps app), 235
dropping pin, 235, 237, 240, 242
DVDs, 173

**E**

earphones, 180
earphones socket, 19
ebooks, 245–247, 249–250, 254
Edit button (FaceTime app), 119

editing
    photos, 211–212
    text, 66
editing features, 104
ellipsis, 61
email
    about, 72, 83, 86, 93–94, 101–111
    account, 94–100, 111
    address, 94, 101
    address book, 83
    attachments, 108
    error message, 104
    folders, 108–109
    to multiple recipients, 102
    notes, 72
    in Notes app, 72
    photos, 204
    signature, 104
    subject line, 103–104
    summary box, 106
    threads, 106
email services, 96–100
Emoji keyboard, 128
encyclopaedia, 70
End Call button (FaceTime app), 121
Enhance button (Photos app), 211
enlarging photos, 141
entering
    information into websites, 144
    website addresses, 136–139
Events option (Photos app), 206
exclamation marks, 59

F

FaceTime app, 22, 25, 36, 86,
    116–122, 254
FaceTime security measure, 117

Featured section (App Store), 218
films, 39–40, 166, 168–171, 189–190
Films option (iTunes store), 166
Find my iPad service, 24
finding where you are, 234
finger marks, 50
finger movements, 1, 20, 25. *See also*
    gestures
5 Live Football Daily, 166
fixing iPad, 50
Flash, 135
flash for photos, 211
flick gesture, 254
focal point, 201, 202
fonts, 55, 56
foreign languages, 61
formatting
    TV shows, 171
    video content, 169, 203, 219
Forward button
    browsing, 144
    iMessage, 128
    Music app, 181, 182
    Videos app, 190
forwarding email, 107
Fotopedia Heritage app, 228
4G mobile communications, 8, 10–14,
    27, 29–33, 48, 136, 241, 253
free
    apps, 194, 217, 219–220, 228, 246
    content, 164, 169, 191, 250
    ebooks, 246, 247, 250
    me.com account, 43, 94
Free button
    iBooks app, 246
    iTunes store, 169, 170
French keyboard, 128
front camera, 8, 120, 201

# G

Game Center app, 25, 228
GarageBand app, 228
GB (gigabyte), 9
General settings, 35, 50, 63, 65, 66, 132, 219
Genius feature, 187, 218
Genres view (Music app), 184, 185
gestures. *See also specific tasks*
   double-tap, 254
   drag, 254
   finger movements, 1, 254
   flick, 254
   for multitasking, 227
   pinch, 141, 256
   slide, 60, 62, 138, 202, 248
   swipe, 86, 105, 128, 153, 165, 170–171, 181, 184, 202, 227
   tap, 257
   tap and hold, 257
Get More Episodes button (Videos app), 190
Get Sample button (iBooks app), 246
getting directions, 237–241
gift certificate, 167
Gmail, 96–98, 194
Go key, 138, 144
Google, 139, 194
Google Contacts, 41
Google Maps, 233, 237–238
GPS, 12
grab point, 68, 154, 249
grey speech bubbles, 128
Guardian Eyewitness app, 228

# H

Harry Potter films, 169
HD (high definition) video format, 169, 203, 219, 254
hearing assistance, 32
Helvetica text style, 56
Hide Keyboard key, 62
high definition (HD) video format, 169, 203, 219, 254
highlighting, 68
History (bookmark folders), 149–150
History folder (Safari web browser), 156
history of website visits, 156
Home button, 18, 254
Home screen, 18, 25, 35, 50, 75, 151, 222, 224–225, 254
host name, 100
Hotmail, 96
hybrid apps, 219
Hybrid map, 234
hyphen, 101

# I

iBooks app, 245–250, 254
iBookstore, 3, 165
iCloud Backup, 46–47
iCloud Control Panel, 45
iCloud service, 10, 17, 22, 24, 37, 42–45, 94–95, 111, 171–172, 174, 205–207, 255
icon, defined, 255
IMAP button, 99–100
iMessage, 126–128, 255
in-app purchases, 219–220
incoming mail server, 100

insertion point, 66–67, 69
installing
  apps, 25, 221
  iBooks app, 246
  software, 37
instant message, 85, 86, 125. *See also*
    iMessage
interactive books, 250
International Keyboards button, 128
Internet connections, 10–14, 21–22,
    27–33
Internet Explorer, 38
iOS 5, 44, 47, 219
iPad. *See also specific topics*
  apps, 219
  capacity, 9, 10, 41
  description, 1–3
  exterior view, 19
  generations, 7–8
  purchase locations, 13–14
  registration, 25
  second-hand market, 8
  set up, 17–25
  software licence agreement, 24
iPhone, 3, 24, 42, 44, 116, 199,
    206, 255
iPhone apps, 218
iPhoto, 43, 44, 205, 206
iPod, 3, 163, 255
iPod touch, 3, 44, 116, 125, 206,
    218–219
iPod touch apps, 218
italic formatting, 104
iTunes app, 25, 173
iTunes icon, 164
iTunes library, 173
iTunes Match, 41, 174–175, 255
iTunes software, 37–39, 48, 255
iTunes status, 39–40
iTunes store account, 167–168, 255

iTunes store secure connection, 23
iTunes Summary pane, 42
iTunes U, 166, 187–188, 189, 191,
    228, 255
ITV Player, 194

## J

jiggling icons, 25, 223, 225, 227
Jobs, Steve (CEO), 164
Johnny Appleseed (John Chapman), 97
Junk email folder, 108

## K

kaleidoscope (photo special effects), 203
keyboards, 59–63, 101, 128–129, 138,
    144
Keychain Access utility, 99
Kindle, 245
Kindle app, 246, 250

## L

landscape mode, 26, 56, 72, 105, 143,
    207, 223, 248, 255
Large Text feature, 34
Last Import folder (Photos app), 206
learning languages, 167
lectures, 187–188
Library button (iBooks app), 247, 250
light tunnel (photo special effect), 203
links
  in ebooks, 249
  on websites, 143–144, 146–147, 155
list manager, 75
lite versions of apps, 220

Load More Messages settings, 110
loading web pages, 138, 143
location of photos, 43–45
location services, 21, 49, 205, 222, 234
locking iPad, 26, 256
locking screen orientation, 35, 227
logging in to FaceTime, 116–117
Looping control (Music app), 185
Lovefilms, 194
LTE symbol, 32

# M

Mac computer, 41, 43–44, 99, 116, 125, 173, 206
magazines, 250–251
magnifying glass, 67–68, 138, 150, 154
Maiden, North Carolina, 46
Mail app, 25, 101, 105–106, 154
Mail icon, 111
Mail Link to this Page (Safari app), 155
Mailboxes button (Mail app), 108–109
managing
    address book, 83–85
    alerts, 130
maps, 21, 234
Maps app, 25, 234–235, 237, 240, 242
Marker Felt text style, 56
marking email as unread, 107
MB (megabytes), 31
Messages, 25
Messages app, 47, 125–126, 130–132
micro SIM card, 11, 13, 27, 29
Microsoft Exchange, 95
mirror effects (photos), 203
mobile broadband number, 29
mobile communications, 8, 10–13, 27, 29–33
MobileMe, 96

modes
    Airplane, 31
    landscape, 26, 56, 72, 105, 143, 207, 223, 248, 255
    portrait, 26, 56, 72, 105, 143, 223, 248, 256
    Private Browsing, 156
    sleep, 26
    video standard, 190
    video widescreen, 190
Mono Audio feature, 34
movies, 39 40, 166, 168–171, 189–190
moving
    apps, 224
    email message, 109
MP3, 175
multiple recipients in iMessage, 128
multipurpose devices, 245
multitasking, 226–227
Multitasking bar, 226–227
music, 39–40, 167–175, 187, 209
Music app, 25, 180
music collection, 63, 174, 180, 187
music on slideshow, 209
Music option (iTunes store), 166
Mute button (FaceTime app), 120

# N

navigating
    App Store, 218
    Home screen, 25
Netflix, 194
New Album button (Photos app), 210
Newsstand, 25, 245–246
Night theme (iBooks app), 249
noises, pinging and whooshing, 111
non-colour effects (photos), 203
Not On This iPad button, 171

Notes app, 25, 71–75, 97
Noteworthy text style, 56
Notification Centre, 77, 130–132, 256
numbers keyboard, 101
numbers on keyboard, 61

# O

O2 (mobile communications), 11, 12, 30
123 key, 61, 62, 101
online shopping. *See* shopping online
Open in New Tab option (website links), 147
Open option (website links), 147
operating systems, 5, 44, 47, 219
Orange (mobile communications), 11
organising
  apps, 222–225
  bookmarks, 152–153
  music, 180
  photos, 205, 209–210
origami (slideshow special effect), 208
outgoing mail server, 100
Outlook software, 45
OX C Lion v.10.7.2, 44

# P

Paint Sparkles app, 228
parental controls, 36
passcode, 36–37
passwords, 21–22, 29, 97, 99, 144
paste feature, 67–69, 104
Pause/Play button (Music app), 180–182
percent sign, 62
photo albums, 209–210
Photo Booth app, 25, 203–204

photo frame, 208–209
photo library, 41
photo special effects, 203–204
Photo Stream, 43–44, 45, 205–207, 213
photo tagging, 200, 205
photo thumbnails, 203–204, 206
photos, 39–40, 88, 141, 200–212
Photos app, 25, 188, 206–213
photos for wallpaper, 154
photos in folders from computer, 206
photos in iMessage, 128
Photoshop Elements, 41, 205, 206
Picture Frame option, 209, 210
pictures in iMessage, 128
pinch gesture, 141, 256
Ping option (iTunes store), 166
pinging noises, 111
Places button (Photos app), 205
playback controls, 180–185, 227
playback speed, 188
playhead control, 182
playhead slider, 190
playing
  audio content, 180–183, 187–188.
    *See also* reading, ebooks
  music, 180–183
  podcasts, 187–188
playlists, 40, 185–187
Playlists button (Music app), 186
Play/Pause button (Videos app), 190
pocket-sized devices, 218
podcasts, 39–40, 170, 187–188, 256
Podcasts option
  iTunes store, 166
  Music app, 187
POP button, 99–100
portrait mode, 26, 56, 72, 105, 143, 223, 248, 256
positioning data on photos, 205
Potter, Beatrix, 250

£ key, 61
power adapter, 49
previewing music tracks, 167
Price button (iBooks app), 246
printing, 72, 107, 155, 235
privacy, 24, 209, 222
Private Browsing mode, 156
pulldown menu, 145
punctuation, 59, 61, 62
Purchased option (iTunes store), 166
push notifications, 221
pushing new email messages with
        iCloud service, 111

# Q

quirky noises, 132
Quote Level formatting, 104
quote marks, 61
QWERTYUIOP keyboard layout, 59

# R

Radio 4's Friday Night Comedy, 166
radio buttons, 145
Reader feature (website content),
        155–156
reading
    ebooks, 247, 249–250
    email, 105–108, 109
    interactive books, 250
    notes, 249
    using iBooks, 247
Reading List, 147, 149–150, 151
rearranging
    apps, 222–226
    web clips, 222–225
receiving FaceTime call, 122

recipes in Notes app, 72
Record button (Videos app), 203
red buttons, 153, 186
Red-Eye button (Photos app), 211
redownloading music/video, 170–172
refurbished iPads, 8
Reminders app, 25, 55, 75–77
removing
    audio content, 170
    bookmark folders, 153
    music, 170–172
    video content, 170–172
replying to email, 107
Reset settings, 35
resetting Home screen, 35, 50
restrictions, 36, 194, 209
Restrictions settings, 36
Retina Display, 8
Review Shots button (Camera app), 202
reviewing photos, 202
ringtone, 86, 122, 166
ripping CDs, 173, 174
Rotate button (Photos app), 211
router, 11, 12, 21

# S

Safari web browser, 25, 135, 145,
        149–151, 155–156, 194, 257
Satellite map, 234
satellite position technology, 233
saving
    draft email, 104
    notes, 55, 58
screen (Retina Display), 8
screen orientation
    app arrangement, 223
    FaceTime, 121
    Notes, 56–57

screen orientation *(continued)*
   photos, 207
   reading ebooks, 247
   reading emails, 105–106
   web pages, 143
screenshot, 200
scrollbar, 142–143
scrolling, 141–143
SD (standard definition) video
         format, 169
Search box, 237–239
searching
   for apps, 218
   in Contacts app, 87
   email, 110
   iTunes store, 167
   in Notes app, 72–75
   for website addresses, 139–140
secure web pages, 146
securing iPad, 36
seeing all recipients in email, 107
Select All button (Photos app), 210
sending
   email, 101–103
   iMessage, 126–128
sensitive information, 146
Sent email folder, 108
Sepia theme (iBooks app), 249
setting preferred language, 21
setting up
   email account with iCloud service, 95
   iPad, 17–25
settings
   Apps, 39–40, 222
   Books, 39–40
   Calendars, 84, 94, 95, 104, 111
   Contacts, 84, 94, 95, 104, 111
   FaceTime, 117, 122
   General, 35, 50, 63, 65, 66, 132, 219
   iCloud services, 42, 46–47

   for impaired vision or hearing, 33–34
   Info, 39–40
   iTunes, 40
   Mail, 84, 94, 95, 104, 111
   Messages, 128
   Mobile Date, 32
   Movies, 39–40
   Music, 39–40, 175
   Notes, 56
   Notifications, 130, 221
   Photos, 39–40
   Picture Frame, 209
   restrictions, 194
   Safari, 156
   sound, 77
   Tones, 39–40
   TV shows, 39–40
   wallpaper, 34, 154
   Wi-Fi connection, 28
Settings app, 25, 38
shaking to erasing, 61
Share Contact button (Contacts app),
         84, 86
sharing
   contact's details in email, 86
   website content, 154–155
shooting video, 203
shopping online
   apps, 221
   books, 246
   iTunes Match, 174–175
   iTunes store, 163–165, 167–169
   using multiple web pages, 145
shortcuts, 65
Show songs on this album button (Music
         app), 184
Shuffle control (Music app), 185, 186
shuffling
   music, 185, 186
   photos, 209

shutter sound, 202
side switch, 35
Silent button, 19
SIM eject tool, 29
SIM tray, 19
simulated thermal camera (photo special effect), 203
16GB iPad capacity, 9, 10
64GB iPad capacity, 9
Skype app, 11
sleep mode, 26
Sleep/Wake button, 19, 26, 27, 256
slide gesture, 60, 62, 138, 202, 248
slider, 20, 27, 122, 190
slideshow, 208–209
Slideshow button (Photos app), 208
Smart Cover, 8, 27, 200, 208
SMS (standard mobile phone text messages), 125
social networking, 155
Social Networking for the Older and Wiser, 136
software
    from App Store, 3
    iTunes, 37–39, 48, 255
    license agreement, 24
    updates to, 8, 38, 44, 47–48, 50, 126, 219
Software Update setting, 47
Songs view (Music app), 180, 183, 185
sound effects, 35, 250
sounds
    for alerts, 77, 119, 122, 132
    for phone ringing, 119
Spam email folder, 108
Spanish keyboard, 128
Speak Auto-text feature, 34
Speak Selection feature, 34
speaker, 180
special characters on keyboard, 60–62

special effects (photos), 203–204, 208
speech bubbles, 128
speech marks, 61
speed, playback, 188
spellchecker, 70
spelling fixes, 69
split keyboard, 129
Spotlight search, 73–75, 90, 101, 223, 256
squeeze (photo special effect), 203
standard definition (SD) video format, 169
Standard map, 234
standard mobile phone text messages (SMS), 125
starting a FaceTime call, 85, 117–119
status bar, 256
storage space
    films, 170
    iCloud, 45
    music collection, 175
    photos, 10
    software and memory, 9–10
    songs, 9
    TV shows, 170
storytelling, future of, 250
Street View button (Maps app), 240
stretch (photo special effect), 203
Subscribe button (iTunes store), 170
subscribing to podcasts, 170
Suggest feature, 70
Swap Cameras button (Camera app), 201
swipe gesture, 86, 105, 128, 153, 165, 170–171, 181, 184, 202, 227
Switch the Badge App icon, 132
symbols on keyboard, 59, 61–62
synchronising
    about, 256–257
    bookmarks, 148, 152–153

synchronising *(continued)*
  calendars, 97
  email, 43, 97
  iCloud with computer, 44–45
  iPad with computer, 39–42, 170
  notes, 43, 97
  photos, 206, 207
  Reading List, 151
  with Wi-Fi, 41–42

# T

tabbed browsing, 145–148
tablet computers, 2
Take Picture button (Camera app), 202
taking photos, 200–203
talking on FaceTime, 121
tap and hold gesture, 257
tap gesture, 257
Terrain map, 234
text size, 249
text styles, 56
32GB, 9, 10
Three (mobile communications), 11
3G mobile communications,
    8, 10–13, 27, 29–33, 48,
    136, 241, 253
thumbnails
  of photos, 203–204, 206
  of videos, 213
tick, 22, 28, 42, 77, 145, 210, 225
tickbox, 77
to-do list (Reminders app), 55
Tomlinson, Ray, 94
tones, 39–40, 132, 166
Top Charts section (App Store), 218
touchscreen, 1, 18, 20, 257
Traffic option (Maps app), 234–235

transitions (photo special effects),
    208, 209
Trash email folder, 108
Trip Advisor app, 228
Triple-click Home feature, 34
troubleshooting, 50
turning
  FaceTime off, 122
  iPad on and off, 26–27
  sounds off, 35
TV Programmes option (iTunes store),
    132, 166
TV shows, 36, 39–40, 168–171,
    190–191, 194
Tweet, 155, 207
twirl (photo special effect), 203
Twitter, 155, 193, 207
typing website addresses with
    keyboard, 138

# U

underline formatting, 55, 104, 107
underscore characters, 101
university lectures, 187–188
unlocking iPad, 20, 27, 257
unread emails, 106
Update Mailbox button (date), 111
updating
  address book, 241–242
  from App Store, 222
  apps, 222
  Reminders app, 47
  software, 8, 38, 44, 47–48, 50,
    126, 219
USB equipment, 37, 38–39, 48
Use photo control (Photos app), 207
usernames, 100, 144

using
  bookmark folders, 152–153
  bookmarks, 152–153
  iTunes on computer, 37–39
  keyboards, 59–62
  Reminders app, 75–77
  Videos app, 189
  Wi-Fi in public places, 136

## V

video, 127, 167–172, 188–191, 203, 213, 254
video calling, 115–116, 121
video content format, 169, 203, 219
video in iMessage, 128
video standard mode, 190
video thumbnails, 213
video widescreen mode, 190
Videos app, 25
viewing
  email attachment, 108
  Home screen, 18
  photos, 202, 205–208
  TV shows, 190–191
  video, 188–191, 213
vision assistance, 32, 33, 140
Vodafone (mobile communications), 11
VoiceOver feature, 32, 65
Volume button, 19
volume control
  alerts, 35
  music, 180–181
  video content, 190
volume indicator and control (Music app), 180–181
Volume settings, 35
Volume Up button (Camera app), 202

## W

wallpaper, 34–35, 154, 207, 257
Wallpaper setting, 34–35, 154
web browsers, 38, 135, 257. *See also* Safari web browser
web clips, 151, 222–226, 257
webmail accounts, 96–98
website links, 143–144
website navigation options, 143
website suggestions, 139
Wells, HG, 250
White on Black feature, 34
whooshing noises, 111
Wi-Fi
  about, 257
  Internet connection, 10–13, 14, 21–22, 27–29
  for Messages app, 125
Wikipedia, 73–74
Windows 7, 44
Windows computer, 37, 43–45, 143, 213
Windows Contacts, 41
Windows Live Hotmail, 96–98
Windows Vista (Service Pack 2), 44
writing
  email, 103–105
  notes, 58–60
www., 136, 137

## X

x-ray (photo special effect), 203

# Y

Yahoo, 96–98
Yahoo address book, 41
Yellow Submarine (book based
    on film), 250
YouTube account, 194
YouTube app, 25, 135, 155, 188, 190,
    191–194, 257
YouTube restrictions, 194

# Z

zoom accessibility controls, 140
Zoom feature, 32
zooming, 140–141, 234